ARCHITECTURE

Publishers of the International Library

LIBRAIRIE ERNEST FLAMMARION—France

VERLAG J. F. SCHREIBER—Germany
(in association with Union Verlag, Stuttgart, and Oster. Bundesverlag, Vienna)

COLLINS PUBLISHERS—Great Britain

RIZZOLI EDITORE—Italy

FRANKLIN WATTS, INC.—United States of America

International Consultants

JEAN-FRANÇOIS POUPINEL—France
Ancien Elève Ecole Polytechnique

KLAUS DODERER—Germany
Professor, Frankfurt

MARGARET MEEK—Great Britain
Lecturer, Division of Language Teaching, Institute
of Education, University of London

FAUSTO MARIA BONGIOANNI—Italy
Professor of Education
at the University of Genoa

MARY V. GAVER—United States of America
Professor Emeritus, Graduate School of Library Science,
Rutgers University

International Editorial Board

HENRI NOGUÈRES

GERHARD SCHREIBER

JAN COLLINS

GIANNI FERRAUTO

HOWARD GRAHAM

INTERNATIONAL LIBRARY

P. M. BARDI

ARCHITECTURE

The World We Build

COLLINS · PUBLISHERS   FRANKLIN WATTS, INC.

London · Glasgow   *New York*

© 1972 International Library
© 1972 Rizzoli Editore

First Edition 1972
ISBN 0 00 100121 3 (Collins)
SBN 531 02104 1 (Franklin Watts)

CONTENTS

CHAPTER 1

THE BUILT ENVIRONMENT

He wished to find out how mankind had been faring—whether its spirit had grown or shrunk. Then he came across a row of newly-built houses, and said, in surprise: What do those houses tell me? No one big in spirit could have put them there, to be in his own likeness! Did some silly child get them out of a box of play-bricks? It's time another child came along and put them back again! Those poky rooms! Can men really walk in and out of them?

Thus spoke Zarathustra, 1892

Why do I start off on this journey into the world of architecture with a quotation from a revolutionary thinker, instead of with the words of some architectural classic like Vitruvius or Le Corbusier? It is because I wish to start the journey here, in the room of a student friend of mine. The floor is covered with books and the walls with posters and magazine pages. The view from the window is of dingy houses, unrelieved by the green of a single tree. Down in the street the roar and the fumes of the traffic make the outdoor environment seem inhuman, while the room itself is stuffy and noisy. This was what brought to my mind the words I have quoted from the German philosopher, Friedrich Nietzsche, referring to the sprawl of 19th-century cities.

This student's room is far from being the worst accommodation you could find in this city where I live, but it has one thing in common with all other rooms, whether in a penthouse, a condemned slum or a prison —they are all architecture. Whoever we are, our lives are affected by built environment, which means that, whether we notice it or not, we are all influenced by architecture.

The relevance of architecture

It is this universal relevance of architecture which gives a meaning to the seemingly random mosaic of posters, magazine pages and advertisements pinned to the wall by my student friend. I have reproduced as the front and back endpapers of this book the "picture wall" as I saw it. Some of the images are gleanings from advertisements or propaganda. Others are of things he believes in, or of things he hates. I wondered what his choice might tell me about his attitude to architecture, and how the building masterpieces of the past are rated by the young people of today.

He approves of the taut structural lines in the rib-vaulting of a Gothic cathedral, but rejects the showy columns of Maderna's Baroque façade on St Peter's, Rome. I notice that he respects simplicity of design (the Mexican pyramid) and functionalism (the suspension bridge). He would like to solve all problems by employing reason (the town-planning scheme). He is impatient to put an end to inequality and injustice (the model and the hungry children), to change a world which means luxury for the few (the formal dining room) and squalor for the vast majority. We see this in the challenging quotation from Le Corbusier, "More guns, more munitions? No thank you! Give us housing, if you please!".

Art gets no special respect, but is treated as part of life. There is one of

A view over the roof tops of Paris from the 12th-century Gothic cathedral of Notre Dame

those disquieting portraits by Francis Bacon, an African woodcarving and some late Picasso brush-drawings. Abstract painting seems to be out, but the influence of abstract art is there, perhaps, in the multi-coloured hand and in the painted stripes on a model's face. The only painter of an earlier age to find a place among these pictures is the 15th-century Hieronymus Bosch, from whose crowded fantasies of pain and pleasure my student friend has picked out a witty detail: we see an old demon-woman melting down a heap of marble capitals in an enormous pan, ready for frying up with what looks like an ostrich egg. So much for architects and their rules of the Classical Orders, in the view of Hieronymus Bosch!

I notice that he is not interested in styles as such. He wants to know what the buildings of the past were for and how they were constructed; to see them in the context of their own times and of the society that paid for them. There is a view of a Mies van der Rohe building, to demonstrate with majestic clarity its designer's dictum that "less is more". There is a photograph of the construction of a native hut somewhere in Africa: he sees more relevance to life in a building project like that than in the skyscrapers soaring up from narrow patches of valuable property in our already overcrowded cities.

As we go along we shall be looking again at this picture wall, to pick up clues to the contemporary view of our architectural heritage. Throughout our journey we will keep asking the question, "Is it relevant to the problems of today?"

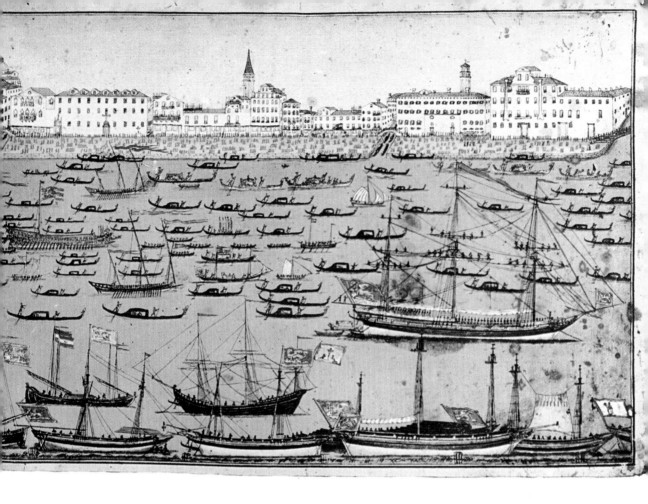

What architecture means

In its widest sense architecture is whatever buildings we live in and work in—the walls that enclose us and the manned capsules we send to the moon are equally structures designed by man for man.

From the first, man built for three main purposes: his own comfort and protection; to provide a setting for religious rites; and to make a home for the dead. And man had to make a start with the materials that nature provides. From using wood, stone and clay, he gradually developed better and more daring techniques until now he works with iron and steel, aluminium, reinforced concrete and plastics.

Progress in the study of early man is slowly building up a picture of the kind of life led by our early ancestors, but it still needs an effort of the imagination to picture to ourselves what life must have been like in a world where there was nothing built or made by man. The forces of nature and the danger from wild animals must have made them very frightened people. Yet it was man who was to win in the end. So the first step on this journey through the world that we build is taken from overhanging ledges of rock and the mouths of caves, where man found natural shelter for himself and his family. Early man adapted these natural shelters to his own use, perhaps by sticking a few branches in the soil, by scraping the earth and moving boulders around. Solving these first problems of construction and function laid the basis for architecture.

Architecture is the practical

The life-blood of Venice – the Basin of St Mark's. In the 16th century Venice was not only a city of artists but also a strong naval and commercial power with strong links with the east, often reflected in its architecture (from an anonymous 16th-century print).

Poets often regard architecture from a sentimental angle – a caricature by R. C. Osborn.

Architectural toys built for his children by Lyonel Feininger, the German-American painter and caricaturist.

Below: Hermann Finsterlin's "style game".

Far below: Design for an educational game with building blocks, devised by Friedrich Fröbel, the creator of the kindergarten system. A former architectural student, he used such games to teach children the meaning of shapes and forms.

arrangement of elements to achieve certain results. Structures and design in architecture keep on developing to meet new requirements and new methods. From the making of a fountain pen to the building of a skyscraper, construction can mean many things. A transistor radio has to be built, and so does a space capsule, and the same process of construction is involved in building a cathedral or putting up a woodman's shelter.

There was a time when architecture was thought of as either Civil or Military (or even Naval). Many of us still have a tendency to think that some types of building are more important than others: that somehow designing a parliament house is a major work, but designing a housing development or a warehouse is only a minor task. The architectural importance of a building does not depend on its features and showiness, nor even on its being built to last. A Maori hut of perishable boards and rushes is just as interesting as a massive Romanesque cathedral. Frank Lloyd Wright's house "Falling Water" can be compared on equal terms with the Parthenon. The entirely functional layout of a nuclear power station can excite the same sort of feelings as the awesome geometry of the pyramids of Egypt.

We must remember that architecture is concerned with constantly changing needs and solutions, and that there is no such thing as correct or incorrect architecture, as was thought in certain periods of history. The German Expressionist architect, Hermann Finsterlin, demonstrated this in an amusing way with the "style game" of building blocks which he brought out during World War I. This was a set of geometrical shapes which could be fitted together to make model buildings in the major architectural styles—Egyptian, Classical, Romanesque, Gothic, Renaissance—at will. The interchangeability of solid forms made the point that there can be no canon of correct and incorrect in design.

Mainly, architecture is a matter of applying human ingenuity to natural materials and to improving upon nature and bringing it under control. From keeping out the rain we have gone on to draining the marshes, damming the rivers, irrigating the deserts. As living conditions in our homes become more and more independent of the climate outside, so our attempts to harness nature grow bolder. While seeking the key to weather prediction and weather control from space stations,

we are planning to harvest the living riches of the oceans. Design and construction—in a word, architecture—touch all these things.

Past and present

Every period has left some public buildings behind it and the world has now become cluttered with buildings, some in ruins, others more or less intact. In the past, earlier buildings of even greater interest than their replacements were torn down to make way for the monuments which we now admire.

Our own age is probably unique in having developed an active conscience about the conservation of historic buildings which we have

A castle being overrun – from a 15th-century illustrated manuscript. Such castles were often complete communities within walls.

From "Linus" 1969

An exercise in rational planning – detail of a beehive.

inherited. This is not just because we have a more informed curiosity about all earlier phases of human history than our forebears did, but because more and more people have come to realize that our history contributes to our environment and that the care and proper use of the buildings we have inherited are as important as providing the new buildings which society needs.

But, unfortunately, deciding whether the new architecture that we get is really what we want, is a much more difficult problem than deciding whether to conserve an old street or redevelop it. Most of us tend to be rather passive about the contemporary buildings we live or work in. We take what we can get, and few of us have any idea of the amount of influence that we, as consumers of architecture, could exert on designers, planners, local authorities and developers. Moves are being made by some government authorities towards public participation in planning, but most of the important decisions which affect our

lives are still being taken in privacy, where the administrative and financial power lies. But the main difficulty is that many people find it hard to express what they really want from the built environment and are therefore no match for the experts.

So it is still a chancy matter whether new developments will be praiseworthy designs that take account of social and environmental values, or be trivial catchpenny schemes. For most of us, the answer will not come until it is too late to do anything about it. And indeed, what standards of judgement should we apply?

In the past there were fashions in architecture when a certain style was dominant, and there were fixed rules to help people to decide what was proper or improper in building. The same decorative style usually ran through all consumer goods— fabrics, furniture, books and paintings. Style was an agreed compromise between the artist and popular taste. The last time when this happened on a large scale in Europe

Mass production in building – a house being constructed from sections prefabricated in the factory then assembled on site. Modern materials and machinery make this the most efficient method of constructing buildings of a standard type.

and America was the phase of Classical revival about the time of the French Revolution.

The Romantic movement, early in the 19th century, brought the search for originality and self-expression. Architecture in the 19th century is a picture of confusion, unlike any previous period in history. From the most varied of motives, architects revived or adapted historical styles, some moving from one to another as their ideas developed. New types of building were required for which there were no precedents, and the resulting solutions were sometimes strange, sometimes brilliant. The story of the Modern movement in architecture belongs to the 20th century, but the ground had been prepared for it by the more creative of the 19th-century movements, from the Gothic revivalists to the practioners of Art Nouveau.

When it comes to judging the very latest trends of our own day in architecture, it is hard to decide what is really significant and valuable. Perhaps we need to know first where our consumer society in the West is going before passing judgement on the architecture of our civilization.

The enormous non-functional bodywork—notably the great aerodynamic fins—which was the fashion on certain American cars a few years ago, and the tempting little suburban dwellings, with period-style features scaled down to suggest some sort of "gracious living", betray the consumer's uncertainty about the proper use of design. The only object of this flashiness and fakery is to sell products on which people might otherwise be reluctant to spend their money. The features which have been superimposed on them are, in a cunning way, rather flattering to prospective buyers. Original thinking in design has a hard fight to win acceptance, when small "Georgian" columns round front porches are felt to represent the respectability and good taste of their owners.

But young people are rejecting this ethic. Wherever there has been student protest in the world, the students of the schools of architecture have played a leading part. They have been protesting not only against out-of-date methods of teaching, but also against the whole way in which our society is organized, against the injustice of a world divided between the prosperous

The synchroton, or electron accelerator, at the Euratom establishment at Saclay in France, is an example of form following function, creating its own kind of beauty.

The design of stacking chairs is a typical designer's exercise. These are "Revolt" chairs by F. Kramer of Holland.

For his design for the entrance to the Illinois Institute of Technology in Chicago, finished in 1940, Mies van der Rohe favoured steel and glass.

industrialized minority and the underdeveloped majority—for they are trained to get down to the essentials. Meanwhile, in the industrialized lands of Europe and North America themselves, millions of people are living in insanitary conditions and substandard housing, while thousands more are homeless.

Looking at buildings

So architecture is many things: it is the design of spaces; the use of materials; planning for society as a whole. It involves respect for the

The industrialization of the 19th century led to the dreadful slums (from a drawing of London slums by the French artist Gustave Doré).

achievements of the past and anticipation of the needs and possibilities of the future. Architecture is also something solid which we, who are not architects at all, see and use and respond to. We should therefore be curious to know how an architect produced such-and-such a result which now stands there for us to criticize. If it has faults, there they are, to be seen and measured. This is the place for a few words on the part of looking at architecture.

A building occupies space in the same way as sculpture or any other object, but architecture has this difference: it also organizes the internal volume of the space; it subdivides it into connecting subspaces, each with a specified function. To an architect, an African grass hut is cylindrical space, topped by a cone to form the roof, and with an opening at ground level to allow the users to go in and out. It presents few constructional problems, all that is needed are natural materials. But already by the Middle Ages, complex structures were required, the realization of which presented serious problems to the designer. For example, the planning of buildings for a medieval community of monks involved the allocation of very large spaces for both the economic subsistence of the community and the performance of their religious duties. To appreciate the success of the design, one has to know how the monks supported themselves, what their rituals were, and how they saw themselves in the society of their time.

Guidebooks and art histories describe thousands of notable buildings, to prepare visitors who are seeing them for the first time. The printed text points out the important features and draws attention as best it can to the spatial qualities of the building. But it takes more than even the most intelligent descriptions or the impressions of a first visit to give a complete understanding of an architectural space. A worthwhile judgement can only be reached by gradually appreciating the formal and functional values which are implicit in the building itself. The Italian architectural historian, Professor Bruno Zevi, advises: "we must put ourselves inside it, we must make ourselves feel a part and a measure of the organism, anything else may be a practical necessity for the purpose of teaching or as an intellectual exercise, but it remains a sheer deception."

Well, we have got to do the best we can here with words and pictures. In the following chapters we will take a look at architecture throughout the world and try to recognize the cases where the designer has used his basic raw material of "space" in an appropriate and imaginative way—in harmony with the natural environment—and those other cases where the designer has simply followed the prevailing rules of style to turn out *pseudo* this or that. Taking examples from the past and the present I will try to show how we can gain a better understanding of the meaning of architecture and see more easily how and why things sometimes go wrong.

Design in the first Machine Age – a pasteboard helmet advertised at the Great Exhibition in London in 1851.

Traditional housing in Afghanistan. There, as in other countries, many people still live in windowless clay huts.

Above: *In San Gimignano in Tuscany, medieval "family castles" are still in good condition.*

Below: *Detail of a Dutch town house in Amsterdam.*

CHAPTER 2

CITIES: BY CHANCE
OR BY PLAN?

Biologically speaking, man's proper habitat is nature, but circumstances long ago forced him to start living in towns. In the advanced industrial countries, more people are urban dwellers than anything else.

If we get out of that student's room and downstairs into the city street, we hurry along the pavements and dash through the traffic like frightened rabbits. City living today makes us tense and jumpy. If we have been lucky enough to get out into the country for a bit, the return makes us even more dissatisfied. We notice more than ever the heavy air, the lack of vegetation, the chlorinated water. Yet while conditions get worse, the influx of people seeking work in the cities is on the increase. The population of some cities is increasing by as much as twenty per cent a year with no plans in existence for coping with the consequences in the future. Other cities have tried to set limits to their growth, with the result that they have had to create whole satellite towns to accommodate their excess population.

The lack of urban planning in the past is now catching up with great cities all over the world, yet the idea of town planning is almost as old as towns themselves. The Romans and the Chinese are famous for the regular and logical pattern on which their towns are laid out. Even the encampment of a Roman legion on the march was a successful exercise in planning on a small scale. But all too often in the past, well-thought-out improvements came to nothing in the face of opposition from people unwilling to change.

An ideal city of our own times, Brasilia—a new capital laid out from scratch—already has its own town-planning problems. When Niemeyer and Costa designed the government buildings and apartment houses of the city centre, they did not reckon with the growth all around them of a ramshackle shanty town to house the construction workers—temporary slums which have now sadly become permanent. Professional town planners have a difficult time, hampered by all sorts of constraints they cannot ignore, regulations and laws, the demands

Town plans over the ages – the common feature of the Roman camp (left) and the fortified Baroque port (right) is the rectangular layout of the streets and squares (from Cattaneo's Quattro primi libri dell architettura, 1554).

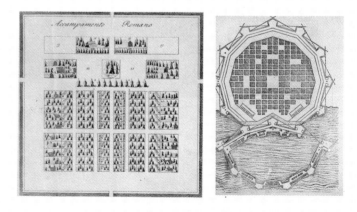

In 1966 two young architects, C. Pelli and N. J. Lumsden, designed this 7,200-home terraced megastructure to be built in the mountains near Santa Monica in California. A foretaste, perhaps, of the cities of the future.

of politics, rapid advances in technology and the pressures of advertising. As a result, the quality of life is steadily being debased.

Ideal solutions

Unfortunately, we cannot simply walk out of our overcrowded, inhospitable cities and build ourselves new ideal communities in more pleasant surroundings, although the wish to take a radical step like this has long been with us. Plato described his ideal city in the 4th

century B.C. In the late Renaissance, Sir Thomas More's *Utopia* had enormous influence in Europe. Robert Owen, the early Socialist, actually put his ideas into practice at New Lanark in Scotland and New Harmony in the United States, although the latter was a failure.

Utopias like these, with the possible exception of the experiment at New Lanark, can be seen as escapist fantasies and offer no practical guidance to the town planner who faces the problems of today. Somewhere this side of Utopia and short of total flight from the chaotic city centres, a solution has to be found.

Part of the answer might be to take all traffic and industry out of the historic core of cities and preserve these intact, for the sake of their picturesque qualities and perhaps as a tourist attraction. Yet, in many European cities there are historic buildings which are teeming with life. People may not want to go. They like their familiar ways and surroundings and we cannot say that they would be happier if they were uprooted and put down in a brand-new satellite town. Many people would prefer to be left alone, however inconvenient their homes may seem to us.

Another city of the future – this one was designed in 1914 by the Italian architect Antonio Sant'Elia and foresees many future developments.

Computer-aided urban planning – sixth-year students in the School of Architecture of Milan University use a computer to draw up a town plan.

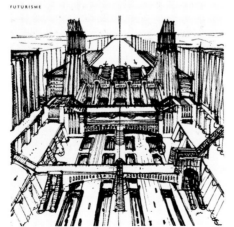

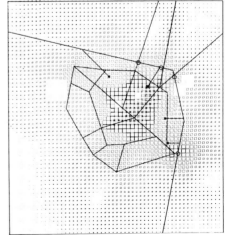

Sunless cities?

If mankind can exist without sunshine and fresh air, supported by carefully calculated "environmental controls", it could have a revolutionary effect on the design of housing in the future. Architects have noticed that science can now keep men alive and useful in the most inhospitable environment imaginable—a capsule in deep space! Some of them are thinking that, with the technology available to us, we must change our ideas about what is necessary for the support of life on this planet.

The schemes of some of these progressive architects, their "plug-in cities" and the like, may appal many people whose idea of good town planning consists of neat lawns, semi-detached houses and a handy shopping centre. But at least these schemes are an attempt to get down to essentials: by examining the purpose of living together in cities at all; by trying to forecast the needs of citizens of the future who will have an increasingly high standard of living and more leisure; by working for economic ways of producing a living environment by employing new resources of materials and power; by asking how long a structure need really last before it should be destroyed and replaced by something newer and better. The schemes they propose may sometimes be closer to science fiction than to even our most advanced building methods, but they are at least making the right approach, they are taking nothing for granted. They are trying to design from facts and not to satisfy ingrained habits and traditions.

Modern town planning is still a very young discipline and we cannot be sure that its practitioners are always able to come up with the right answers. An enormous amount of data is available to us, both on present-day city conditions throughout the world and on how cities came into being, developed and at last nearly suffocated themselves. In computers we have powerful means of turning this data into meaningful patterns from which we may learn yet more. There is some hope to be gained from the fact that computers give us a far greater capacity than we have ever had before for the sheer handling of the vastly complicated calculations which are necessary if we are to read future trends correctly from the evidence of what is happening now.

Below left: *The saltworks and model village at Arc-et-Senans, near Besançon, were designed by the French Classical architect Claude-Nicolas Ledoux and built between 1775 and 1779. Only fragmentary parts of this romantic yet practical work remain, but these have recently been restored by the French government.*

Below right: *Housing for construction workers on the Juquià Dam on the Paranà river in Brazil is also a pilot scheme for a new town of 15,000 inhabitants*

Above: *The round houses of the inhabitants of Elmolo Island on Lake Rudolph in Kenya are made of branches and leaves.*

Below: *A prehistoric village on stilts was reconstructed on Lake Constance in 1929.*

CHAPTER 3

THE ARCHITECTURAL
MINIMUM: A HUT

There are no such things as "sophisticated" architecture and "plebian" architecture. The only judgements that can be made are based on the quality of materials used and on fitness for function. The function can change rapidly from what was intended when the building was designed, but if we still like the building in its new use, then it still has fitness.

In this survey we shall come across many types of building, but no "mere" building. The simplest kind of building is a hut. There was a time when the only people to take an interest in how huts were constructed were the anthropologists, but the Austrian historian Rudofsky changed all that with his book *Architecture without Architects*. Anthropology itself is held in respect now by many architects who feel they have much to learn from the study of communities that have been little touched by Western civilization.

The simple life is a matter which I myself know a good deal about, for my home is in one of the countries of the Third World—South America— where the local buildings are very modest, for the simple reason that the people cannot afford them to be otherwise. Their inhabitants know a lot about life and have plenty of common sense, even though they have little experience of

the benefits of industrial progress. Their ways will begin to change, of course, as new products become available and they begin to feel the powers of persuasion upon them. Their old framework, handed on for generations, will crumble and break and fail them. The merchandisers of material benefits will not be interested in this. A new market is all that matters. This may not be very attractive but it is a fact of life, and it is perhaps not an oversimplification to say that this is the way in which we spread Western civilization.

The Bororo's huts

Not many of the primitive buildings —archaic buildings would be a better description—that are still in use will survive contact with our civilization. Most of them are destined to disappear without trace. In a few remote places of the Third World such buildings are still being made. In the Amazon forest I have watched a tribal hut being put up. It is a large rectangular structure which will be used exclusively by adolescent boys. In their tribal society custom requires them to spend this time away from the generation of their parents. They know that when they reach the prescribed age they will be accepted by the tribe as adults. They live here in a way not

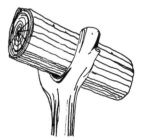

A hut made of logs and bark (from a 19th-century Italian drawing).

The origin of the "capital" – an upright branch supporting a beam.

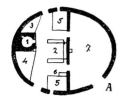

unlike some commune of poor students pooling their resources in order to live cheaply. When the initiation ceremonies and feasts are over, they hand over their club house to the next generation of boys. The new adults go on to other huts to live a life of obvious mental and physical maturity. These Bororo people of the Amazon lead an archaic but far from primitive existence. The huts they build are of two types, one according to each season: a cone-shaped, enclosed structure for the dry months; and a rectangular, spacious one with a palm-thatched roof for the rainy season.

The drop-out way of life in our

Western civilization is in many ways far more impoverished than the life of these Amazonian Indians, but it does reflect an awareness among young people of the West that there are other human values besides those which make modern urban existence possible. In much the same way, the minimum architecture of the Bororo adolescents' hut is an indictment of the values which are implicit in the vast structures that house the Saturn space vehicles on Cape Kennedy. For we must not forget that a hut, whether built of sticks and mud, or kerosene tins and packing cartons nailed together, is still the only expression of the art of

building for at least a thousand million human beings.

Structural simplicity

The building of huts is of two main types: the rectangular, post-and-beam form and the hemispherical form constructed of concentric circles. The first type tends to be built of timber, with strong upright beams and a pitched roof covered with whatever local plant product is most likely to keep out the rain. The hemispherical type tends to be a more elastic structure, probably consisting of supple twigs woven together to form a network with the ribs, which are first planted in a circle in the ground and then bent inwards and joined together at the crown, forming walls and roof in one. When mankind later started to build with stone, these two types of hut provided the constructional model for the rectangular temple with pillars (Egypt and Greece) and for the beehive tomb (Mycenae) and later the dome itself (Rome). Indeed,

The North American Prairie Indians were nomads and therefore lived in tents.

A gold prospector in his log cabin, 1866 (from a painting in the Museum of Fine Arts, Boston, Massachusetts).

All over the world there are such shanty towns on the outskirts of large cities.

An Eskimo igloo village (from La Terre et les mers by Louis Figuier, 1864).

primitive hunters living under Arctic conditions—the Eskimos—learned to handle blocks of ice as if they were masonry, and became skilled builders of dome igloos. The cut and fit of the blocks is as precise as the work of a Roman engineer.

Influence on later buildings

Many details of the carpentry in the earlier timber buildings, especially in the way the uprights met horizontal members, were carried over into stone buildings, as carved copies of the original joints. The tradition was so strong that it conditioned the decorative form of capitals right down to the end of the Classical period.

The tent is one ready-made, fold-away type of building that seemed until recently to have no influence on the architecture of sedentary civilizations. Nowadays, many millions of people become nomads against their will, and the use of the tent to house hordes of refugees, whether from natural disasters like earthquakes and floods or from political upheavals, has unfortunately become a familiar sight. And in the last few years, some architects and engineers have seen the advantages in being able to construct tent-like structures to cover enormous areas and thousands of people for a temporary need, such as an exhibition or a big sports event. In this way the lessons of even the lightest and most temporary of human buildings, the nomad's tent, have been learned and applied by modern technology.

An Indian peasant weaving leaves into the framework of a temporary hut put up near the rice paddies of Shivpuri.

CHAPTER 4

THE AGE OF STONE

For a period of perhaps half a million years early man, in order to survive, made use of the natural shelters available to him. Eventually, however, as his awareness grew, he developed stone tools to the point where he could work the natural materials around him, cutting down timber to build huts. From there it was only a matter of time to the development of more sophisticated tools and the ability to work with stone.

As far as we know, what prompted man to build with stone was not a desire to replace the frail wooden or mud structures in which he lived by stronger and more permanent ones, but his wish to make his ritual religious precincts more permanent, such as a sacred grove or the wooden posts of a temple enclosure. The advent of the early Bronze Age in the Mediterranean and western Europe is marked by the erection of megalithic monuments—huge blocks of stone usually placed in a circle. These standing stones, some of astonishing size, often had to be moved—as at Stonehenge, where there are traces of three different monuments—over great distances. Sometimes the stones were placed upright in their natural state, sometimes they were quite skilfully dressed with stone hammers. Tomb chambers, set around the stone circle, and the passages leading to

them, had to be walled and roofed strongly enough to withstand the load of earth on top. Thus, in the service of the dead, many basic engineering problems were solved. The flat stone laid on two uprights, still to be seen in Brittany, Ireland and elsewhere, where they are known as *dolmens*, is what remains of the burial chamber itself after the earth has been washed away.

Although houses built of stone did not appear until much later, the architecture of domestic wooden buildings was making progress. Well-built huts could now stand in safety above the surface of lakes, supported by piles driven into the lake bed below and away from the dangers lurking on the shore. This kind of construction is still in use in parts of Asia and Africa.

Artificial caves also have a place in the history of the development of stone as a building material. The skills necessary for mining into the rock, disposing of the rubble and making the interior safe must have added to man's knowledge of the quarrying and dressing of masonry.

Tools for stone

The available tools seem to have been stone axes and wooden wedges and, for moving large standing stones, artificial sloping ramps with, perhaps, tree trunks as rollers. Un-

This megalithic sculpture in Valletta Museum, Malta, is that of a mother-goddess figure.

Opposite above:
Artist's impression of how Stonehenge probably looked.

Opposite below:
Cave dwellings at Noto on the island of Sicily.

27

Above: *Medieval monasteries were carved out of the volcanic rock at Göreme on the Anatolian plateau of Turkey.*

Above right: *About 3,000 giant menhirs, set out in long rows, stand in the neighbourhood of the little town of Carnac in Brittany.*

Below: *The cave village of Guadix in Andalusia is partly inhabited to this day.*

limited patience and manpower must have been available. Even so, it is clear from the plan of megalithic sites that their builders knew exactly what they wanted when setting out their avenues, circles and enclosures. Considering the mechanical difficulties, their success in achieving symmetry, balance and structural strength is quite remarkable. The ability to fit together uneven blocks of enormous size, without cement, in fortified walls that have lasted for thousands of years, can be seen not only in the cyclopean masonry of western Europe, but also in the pre-Inca cities of the Andes.

Inventing the arch

Experiments were made, and by finding new ways of tilting, leaning or stacking stones of various sizes, it became possible to build higher retaining walls and to roof over larger spaces than previously. By propping two shorter stones together, with their ends meeting at an angle in the centre, where formerly a long lintel stone had been laid flat across the tops of two uprights to form a doorway, the most daring of Stone Age builders found they could construct an entrance

The 3,000-year-old frieze of the Stone Age temple of Hal Tarxien in Malta has a double-spiral decoration in relief and was originally coloured.

Below: *An echo of the megalithic style in the Mediterranean — 19th century Turkish gravestones at Izmir.*

that not only gave greater head clearance, but also supported the load above it by distributing the thrust down to the uprights. The old lintel stone had carried the load along its whole length, with the danger of splitting in the centre if there were any weakness in the slab used.

The "beehive"

If some of the higher blocks in a stone wall are longer and allowed to jut out from the face of the wall, they can be used to support more blocks or wooden beams on top. These jutting blocks are called *corbels* and are the foundation of yet another important technical advance. The Stone Age builders found that if they built a stone wall in the form of a circle, treating each course of blocks above a certain height as corbels, and continued to build inward, with each circular course of corbels smaller than the one below, they would eventually have a sort of beehive-shaped cupola, closing at the top. These structures were widely used in the Mediterranean area in the Bronze Age period. Even today they are traditionally used in remote areas of

The Incas built the walls of their capital city, Cuzco, in Peru from huge pieces of rock.

the Balkans and Sardinia where they are known as *trulli*.

Then it must have occurred to someone to combine the ideas of the leaning-slab doorway and the corbelled roof. In temples of the pre-Columbian Maya civilization of Central America, we can see how this was done. At the top of the pillars of stone, courses of masonry were corbelled inwards over the opening until they met at the centre, leaving a triangular space above the level of the top of the pillars. This triangular "arch" was strong enough to carry massive walls above. The idea was even developed into a wedge-shaped passage rising directly from floor level.

These were steps in the progress towards the discovery of the true arch and, through that, of the principles of vaulting.

Substitutes

Stone began to replace timber for many purposes, and its strength and durability increased its importance as a building material. In lands where wood was scarce, such as the Nile Valley, its use became widespread, but everywhere the feeling grew that really important buildings, the ones that had to last—temples, tombs, citadels and palaces—must be built or rebuilt in stone.

Another important substitute for timber was discovered when it was found that if small shaped slabs of mud or clay were dried in the heat of

The *trulli* is a prehistoric building form which is still used in the Apulia region of Italy.

the sun or of a fire the result was the brick, one of the most versatile building inventions of all time. It is still in use everywhere in the world today, five or six thousand years after its first appearance in Mesopotamia and Egypt.

Modern "stone"

A derivative of stone, which has almost entirely supplanted it in 20th-century architecture, is con-crete. Successfully used by Roman engineers, concrete was revived and improved by early 19th-century chemists. Almost infinitely malleable in its applications, modern concrete is a compound of powdered rocks and minerals, silica, alumina and lime. Without the range of possibilities offered by modern concrete, especially when reinforced by steel bars, the "new architecture" of the 20th century could hardly have developed.

A dolmen in the menhir region near Carnac. The earth of the covering mound of this passage-grave has been washed away.

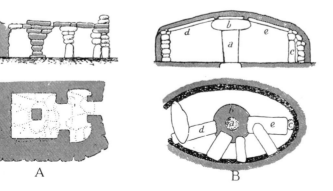

A

B

Plan of a megalithic corbel-roofed structure in the Balearic Islands. The drawings show developments in vaulting.

CHAPTER 5

CIVILIZATION
MEANS CITIES

Man had been building for centuries before he started writing. But as soon as records began to be kept, during the second millenium B.C., we can find out what mankind had been up to: migrations, plunder, conquest, the restless doings of ambitious and ruthless chieftains, all punctuated with the natural disasters of flood, earthquake and volcanic eruption. We do not know where it all started, but the human game was in full swing about 5000 B.C. in the Middle East. We find groups and populations in rivalry with one another for the honour of their gods or the rights of their kings, and bound together in social organizations which laid down the legal, moral and religious government of their lives. Of these aspects, the religious had the greatest influence.

Relationships with the spirits were vital at every point of daily life and the supernatural was taken for granted. Life was but a passing phase, death was the everlasting reality. Realms were born, flourished and died; invaders appeared, ravaged and vanished; civilizations grew, some to extraordinary heights

Above left: *An artist's impression of an Egyptian temple.*

Left: *The terraced Step Pyramid of the Egyptian king Zoser at Saqqara was built about 2950 B.C. and is the first large structure of stone known in history.*

of refinement, and then collapsed into inertia, in some places other rougher peoples taking over their knowledge and forging from it something more lasting.

By the second millenium B.C., the foundations of the future had been laid on the banks of certain great rivers of Afro-Asia: Chinese civilization on the Yangtze Kiang; Indian civilization on the Indus and the Ganges; Mesopotamian civilization between the Tigris and the Euphrates; and Egyptian civilization on the Nile. The Mediterranean —"frogs' pond" as Plato called it— and untamed Europe above it, were full of traders and raiders, pirates and tribes on the move.

In the river civilizations, the emphasis was on order, on religious and social discipline, with priests and kings (sometimes the same person) at the top. The identity of state and religion was often expressed in architecture. Temple structures at the cultural centres were used to express, by their sheer mass and imposing proportions, the timeless and indestructible nature of a divinely-ordained society, and gigantic sculptures of figures, part-human, part-animal, played on the people's fear of the beasts.

By comparison, the civilization which developed later around the shores of the Aegean and its islands, seems far more pleasant. Mythology

An Egyptian leafy capital.

An Egyptian gilded bronze statuette of Queen Karomana (XXII dynasty), in the Louvre, Paris.

The Temple of Amon at Luxor, built in 1400 B.C. by Amenophis III – the sanctury (left) and the colonnade (right).

and life were in a more harmonious relationship with each other, feelings were gentler and behaviour more humane. It was an atmosphere more favourable to those aspects of civilization which we value today.

The Nile Valley

To live in peace and plenty, the Egyptian peasants required the

waters of the Nile to rise and fall at certain seasons. Nature was not always obliging, so the magical powers invested in the god-priest-king, the Pharaoh, and invoked hopefully to produce rain, had a desperate importance in everyday life. But the Pharaohs themselves had another obsession—the idea of immortality. To satisfy the demands of rituals that held the living in the vice of the hereafter, the Pharaohs imposed on their people a programme of building and maintenance, the physical and emotional costs of which were to prevent the people of the Nile Valley from ever having a chance to develop the free and independent character of the later Hellenic civilizations.

The mathematical precision and subtlety of form of ancient Egyptian work has rarely been attained in any period since. Yet among the pyramids, the colossal figures, the temples, the rock-hewn tombs, we find no spectacular dwellings for the Pharaohs themselves. The state they maintained at the altars, or as mummified corpses, was what mattered, their passing domestic

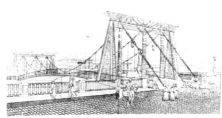

Egyptian forms used in the West to express strength – in Philadelphia Jail (above), and in a design for a bridge (below). The interest in Egyptian forms became particularly strong after Napoleon's expedition to the Nile in 1798–99.

life on earth was unimportant. The roles of architect and building craftsman merged with that of the priest.

Convention became all-important. Construction, and the complementary decorative paintings, reliefs and sculptures, had to be reproduced faithfully and without error from the sacred models handed down from the past. Innovations there certainly were over the centuries, but always within what was

The funeral temple of Queen Hatshepsut (XVIII dynasty) was built on three terraces at Deir el Bahri about 1500 B.C.

The erection of the obelisk in St Peter's Square, Rome, in 1586. The drawing gives an idea of the engineering problems which the Egyptians themselves must have faced when it was first built in 37 B.C.

Steers decorate a capital in the palace of Artaxerxes II, built in the 4th century B.C., in Susa in Iran.

A Mesopotamian statue of Gudea, a Governor of Ur in the third millenium B.C.

Left: Reliefs carved on the north stairway of the Palace of Darius I (the Great) at Persepolis, date from the 6th century B.C.

Right: The tomb of Darius II at Naqsh-i-Rustam. The façade represents a palace and it was built in 404 B.C.

felt to be a timelessly valid framework of religious practices.

This aspect has sometimes tempted Western architects to use the form of ancient Egyptian temples to lend dignity to contemporary secular buildings—often with bizarre results. A feature which has fitted more easily into the unlikely surroundings of Western capital cities is the obelisk, many of which were transplanted to various European and American cities, particularly in the 19th century. The super-obelisk commemorating George Washington in the United States' capital is a tribute to the power this sophisticated form of the standing stone still has on the civilized imagination.

The first cities

The first real towns appear to have come into existence about seven thousand years ago in the hills of the Middle East, in the area we now know as Turkey, Syria, Iraq, Lebanon and Israel. From that time onwards, the history of Mesopotamia (now Iraq) and the adjoining lands became the history of cities—of people whose lives were formed by a built environment.

The chariots of conquerors swept over these cities from every side, but life went on. A site may have been abandoned and forgotten, like Sumer, but some other city would take its place, demonstrating the immense continuity of living cities. It may be unnatural, but it has gone on being unnatural without a break for an extremely long time!

Babylon and Sumer

Babylon was one of the greatest cities in the ancient world. It has disappeared now, but first Seleucia, then Ctesiphon (about 55 B.C.) and lastly Baghdad (founded A.D. 762), all near to the site of old Babylon,

Above: *Artist's impression of a ziggurat. Thirty-three such step towers have been excavated in Mesopotamia ("the land between the rivers").*
Below: *Reconstruction of the entrance gate to the town of Nineveh.*

carried on its role as key city of Mesopotamia.

The main building material of Mesopotamia was ceramic, that is brick faced with coloured tiles. This method was used because the only stone quarries were in hostile hands, far away in the hills, and timber was scarce—so scarce that the bricks were not fired in wood-burning kilns, but baked under the sun.

The pyramid-building urge was as strong in the Mesopotamian culture as in those of ancient Egypt and pre-Columbian South and Central America. But where, to the Egyptians, a pyramid was a gigantic strong-box, protecting a coffin at its centre, in Mesopotamia it took the form of the *ziggurat*—a brick-built, stepped hill, with a temple at the top. In America the stone pyramids seem to have been of both types in different regions.

The strength of buildings was considered all-important, and this was achieved by the massive use of sun-baked brick, fixed in a mortar of bitumen. Just to make sure that they got their calculations right, any architect/builder whose building collapsed lost his life.

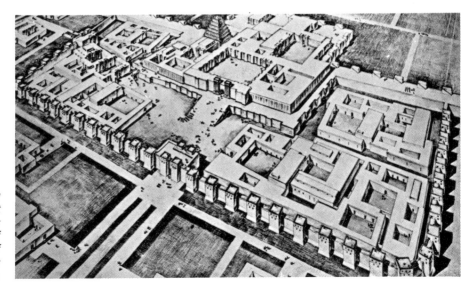

Following excavations at Khorsabad, this reconstruction of the Assyrian city of Dur Sharrukin was made.

The enforced use of brick had one particular advantage—because of its flexibility of structural form, it became possible to build rounded arches and then vaults, some of them of stupefying size, like the great hall of Ctesiphon.

The main reason that so little Mesopotamian architecture has survived is war. Incessant war between dynasties ruined the cities. Devastations by invading hordes ruined the economy, which depended on keeping the intricate system of irrigation channels working. Much of the fertile land turned into desert. With lack of care, the massive brick walls crumbled and the exposed brickwork was scrubbed away by the wind-borne sand.

Iran

Meanwhile, in the mountains and highlands to the east of the Tigris-Euphrates plain, another civilization of cities had come into being during the fifth millenium B.C. These were the cultures of Iran, produced by a mixture of peoples who came into the area at different times and from different directions, but all of them owing a good deal to the Sumerian, or early Mesopotamian, civilization.

There was plenty of timber in Iran in ancient times and no shortage of quarries in the hills. The building forms were therefore often executed in stone, while keeping suggestions of more ancient timber constructions, with slender columns supporting beams and lintels. Like the Egyptian Pharaohs, the kings of ancient Iran were often buried in magnificent tombs carved deep in the rock face. Even here, the sculptured façade outside would be a faithful imitation of a three-dimensional columned building with roof and pediments.

The elegant ruins of Persepolis, the palace-capital of the Iranian "King of Kings", built by the king Darius the Great in the 6th century B.C., now stand isolated in the middle of a dusty plain. They are a monument to the destructiveness of what we call civilization, for this "Iranian Versailles" was burnt to the ground by Alexander the Great, who carried classical Greek culture and its artistic and architectural traditions to the whole of the Near and Middle East, and even as far as India.

Glazed brick was the material used for this relief of a lion in the palace of Babylon.

The remains of a house at Hassmabad in Iran. It was made of dried mud bricks.

A Minoan capital
from Knossos.

Crete and the Aegean

However nomadic their prehistoric, tribal ancestors may have been as they wandered through south-eastern Europe towards the Mediterranean, the Greeks quickly adopted the urban life. The building of cities became the hallmark of ancient Greek civilization, and wherever they spread as colonists, the first act of the Greeks was to found a new city. Local chieftains built strongholds, such as Mycenae, Argos and Tiryns. Later, the centres of their cultural, religious and political life shifted to those more open settlements whose names still symbolize the meaning of "civilized city": Athens, Thebes, Corinth, Ephesus, and so on.

The ruins of the Bronze Age civilization of Mycenae in ancient Greece were first uncovered in the 1870s by Heinrich Schliemann, the discoverer of the site of Troy. Consisting mainly of fortifications surrounding storehouses and royal tombs, they were built of such massive masonry that it seems amazing to us that the Mycenaeans were able to manoeuvre the huge

A baked and
painted clay figurine
of a goddess from
Cyprus (now in the
Archaeological
Museum, Florence).

These passage walls
in the citadel of
Tiryns, were built of
limestone blocks
over nine feet high.

blocks into position and make them fit together so firmly. There are corbel-roofed passages within the walls and tapering, beehive-shaped tombs, all of which were built without a knowledge of the true arch.

Mycenaean building skills can be seen in the well-preserved *tholos*, or "beehive" chamber tomb, at Mycenae itself, which was dubbed the Treasury of Atreus. A long passage leads to a rectangular stone doorway, beyond which was the main circular chamber buried in the hillside. It is a pointed dome springing from the ground and constructed of stone corbels laid in concentric courses diminishing towards the top. At right angles to the entrance a smaller door leads into a side chamber.

About the beginning of the 12th century B.C., the start of the Iron Age in Greece, the Mycenaean culture collapsed in its turn, possibly overrun by the final wave of Greek migrants, the Dorians.

Impressive though these robust beginnings of classical Greek architecture may be, they are coarse and clumsy compared with the achievements of the civilization which existed on Crete for some fifteen hundred years *before* the Mycenaean Greeks established their supremacy.

Minoan civilization

The dramatic rediscovery of the Minoan civilization by Sir Arthur Evans, the British archaeologist, dates from only 1899.

Forgotten until then, this earliest of European civilizations can now be seen, from the architectural and artistic evidence, to have achieved a high level of peaceful culture before disappearing about 1400 B.C., overwhelmed perhaps by some volcanic disaster. Its artists' playful sense of form and colour in the surviving frescoes and pottery can still enchant us, and the drainage system in the palace of Knossos is evidence that the Minoans had civil engineers whose equals are not found again until the time of the Romans.

Knossos and Phaistos, the two main centres of the Minoan civilization, contain sumptuous building complexes to provide for the needs of a whole community. The build-

Mycenae as it probably looked about 1500 B.C. It was a fortified citadel with the palace at the top.

Gold model of a temple façade, found by Schliemann in a Mycenaean tomb.

The Palace of Knossos on Crete. The partially restored portico of the north entrance (above), and the South Propylon with procession frescoes (below). Building activity at Knossos lasted until 1400 B.C. with repeated extensions and restorations.

ings did not have many storeys, but achieved an impression of height by being built on terraces stepped one behind the other. The massive columns, the walls of the porches and of the rooms inside were all covered with delicately-painted decorations showing animals, especially bulls, athletic young men and women, flowers, birds and countless spirals. The courtyards lay at different levels, with pillared loggias giving onto the open air investing Minoan architecture with an open and luminous quality which contrasts with the later solid architecture of the Mycenaeans.

The megaron and its successors

The Mycenaeans built no temples, but one of the most common types of building was the chieftain's hall or *megaron*, a rectangular building with a pitched roof, a hearth in the centre and with a pillared portico and a small antechamber at one end. At the close of the Greek Dark Ages, from about 1100 to 900 B.C., in the

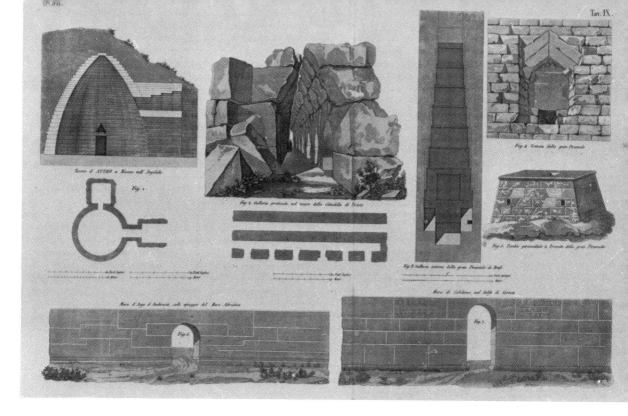

"archaic" period of Greek art, this kind of building came to be adopted as a suitable habitation for the carved figures of the gods and goddesses of Olympus. In this way, the foundations for the classical Greek temple, with its portico of columns and its inner chamber containing a statue of a god, were modelled on a Mycenaean house.

Small votive shrines to begin with, in which the offerings brought by pilgrims to the home of the god could be kept, they were built of wood and mud bricks. By the 7th century B.C., temples were larger and built of stone, the essential plan and construction still being based on the wooden members of earlier buildings. The details were embodied in a set of rules which were known as the Doric Order, the earliest of the three Classical orders of architecture which have been handed down to us, and which for many centuries dominated—and sometimes paralysed—the imagination of European architects.

Drawings of Mycenaean building techniques by Rondolet. The Mycenaean culture knew the principle of the vault and the arch.

The west court and grand staircase of the Minoan palace at Phaistos on Crete. This area was probably used for theatrical or religious purposes

An Etruscan grave structure of the 3rd century B.C. at Cortona in Tuscany.

An Etruscan capital.

The Etruscans

By the 8th century B.C., there were movements of peoples in the central Mediterranean area which were to have a great influence, centuries later, on the kind of architecture and culture which the Romans were to carry with them on their conquests. The Etruscans settled in the Italian peninsula, in the region which is still called after them, Tuscany. It is almost certain that they came there by sea, and probable that their earlier home was in Asia Minor, although nothing is known of their origin or of the reason for their migration. By about 500 B.C., they had extended their dominion to nearly the whole of Italy, the spread of their power owing much to trade, to their well-organized agriculture and to their mastery of iron-working, much of it absorbed from the more developed lands of the eastern Mediterranean.

A strange and complex people, whose language is still undeciphered, the Etruscans were famed as diviners and were ruled by a religion of dark rites, some of which the Romans were to inherit. They buried their dead in cave-like tombs cut in the volcanic tufa of the region. Later

Plans of Etruscan buildings – the Tomb of the Shields at Tarquinia (right) and of a temple (far right). The Etruscan tomb had the ground plan of a house, and the temple is surrounded by columns.

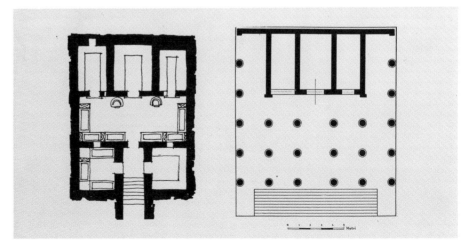

forms had a number of chambers with painted walls or even reliefs in plaster, illustrating subjects that were common in the decoration of Greek pottery which was much imitated in Etruria. The dead were provisioned with food offerings, and to amuse them the wall decorations recorded scenes of magic and incidents from everyday life.

The Romans destroyed most Etruscan buildings, but we know what Etruscan houses looked like from the clay models they were fond of depositing in tombs. They were oval or rectangular in plan, several storeys high, and built of wood, rubble or clay on a frame of timber or masonry.

During the 7th century B.C., Etruscan cities flourished on the site of earlier small centres. They were built on a square plan of Hellenic type, around a capitol containing temples to their gods. Outside the walls stood the cities of the dead, dominating the living from their great hill-like *tumuli*, or burial mounds.

Although they had close contacts with the Aegean and copied much Greek art, the Etruscans did not imitate the Greek orders of architecture. They seem to have created a simple and primitive version of their own, which was later taken over by the Romans and became known as the Tuscan Order.

Because of their assured and technically advanced use of the arch, at one time it was thought that it was an Etruscan invention, but its origins are now known to date back to Mesopotamia.

Above left:
Volterra in Tuscany still lies partly behind Etruscan walls whose south gate is decorated by three mysterious heads.
Above right:
In Alatri, south-east of Rome, the 4th-century B.C. pre-Roman wall, constructed of polygonal masonry and with a stone lintel sixteen feet long, still stands in almost perfect condition.

This 5th-century B.C. Etruscan tomb from Casal Marittimo has a corbelled circular roof and a central pillar which is non-supporting (now in the Archaeological museum, Florence).

CHAPTER 6

THE ACHIEVEMENTS
OF THE GREEKS

The term "Greek Architecture" almost certainly brings to mind a picture of the Parthenon. And the Parthenon, as we all know, is one of the high points of architecture of all time. But what relevance can it possibly have for architects faced with the problems of today? Indeed, what does the Parthenon mean to us, other than as a sightseeing goal?

To attempt to answer these questions, let us start with the meaning of the words themselves: the *Parthenon* on the *Acropolis* of *Athens*. "Parthenon" means the *virgin goddess's shrine*; "Acropolis" means *hightown*, the name for the fortified settlements which the Greeks built at the top of rocky crags; "Athens" is the city dedicated to the virgin goddess *Pallas Athene*, the goddess whose image stood in the Parthenon.

Here we have some clues: the Parthenon was the chief temple of the most important and most advanced city in the Greek world and represented the best that Greek art and civilization could produce. In its own time (it was built between 447 and 432 B.C.) and until the end of the Classical world, it ranked as the supreme achievement of the

Above left: *An artist's impression of the Acropolis in Athens as it was in the 5th century B.C.*
Left: *The Doric temple of the Parthenon on the Acropolis, as it is today*

Doric Order in architecture and was never surpassed.

The type of building it was based on—the megaron—links it with the beginning of human settlements in towns, while its use as the religious centre of civic, political and cultural life links it with great cities of the future.

Doric, Ionic and Corinthian

The architects of the Parthenon, Callicrates and Ictinus, made skilful and subtle use of the proportions of the Doric Order—the earliest of the three Greek architectural orders and based on the proportions of the Doric column—and these unique qualities of the Parthenon, even in its shattered state today, can be seen by comparing it with other Doric structures at Delphi, Cape Sounion, Agrigentum and Paestum.

But in purely technical terms, a study of the Parthenon will solve no problems for the modern architect. It offers no model for any building type that an architect will be called upon to plan today, and its decorative motifs and friezes have no place in modern construction methods. Yet, because of its superb fitness of function and beauty of form, the Parthenon stands as a supreme example of the architect's role in the context of society and of his potential both as a builder and

The three Greek capitals –Doric, Ionic, Corinthian.

The bronze charioteer at Delphi.

as an artist. This is what gives the Parthenon its relevance, even after two thousand four hundred years.

The two other orders of architecture used by the Greeks were the Ionic—named after the eastern islands and cities of the Aegean Sea and Asia Minor where it originated in the 6th century B.C.—and the Corinthian of the 5th century B.C., named after the city of Corinth. The Ionic was less hampered by memories of the old, robust timber construction than the Doric Order had been, and gave a lighter, more delicate impression, showing more truly the load-bearing capacity of masonry with its thinner columns. Corinthian was the last and most decorative order, and was the one which the Romans later adopted so vigorously. It combines the slenderness of the Ionic with strong reminiscences, in its leafy capitals, of primitive building methods.

The round temple on the Marmaria terrace at Delphi was built in the early 4th century B.C.

The Doric temple of Poseidon at Cape Sounion was built in the mid 5th century B.C.

The Greek city

By the time the Parthenon in Athens was completed, architecture in the Greek city states had made tremendous progress, but it was still applied only to the great religious sanctuaries. Houses were simple and built of mud-brick and timber.

Then, in the century that followed, when the power of the city states was declining as the result of civil war and the rise of the Macedonian empire, a period of great architectural activity began. Stone theatres were built, the loveliest of the surviving ones being probably the theatre of Epidaurus, built about 350 B.C., with its elegantly geometrical plan and its marvellous acoustics. New towns were laid out on a rational grid pattern, streets were paved and good drainage became the rule. Buildings for specifically civic uses were built.

The Hellenistic world

When the Greek style of life spread
to the Middle East and to Egypt in
the wake of the armies of Alexander
the Great, these town-planning
skills were adopted in the Hellenized
kingdoms forming Alexander's empire. The great city of Alexandria in
Egypt was a new foundation, built
to a Greek grid plan, and other,
lesser cities scattered across Afro-
Asia all boasted their markets,
theatres, stadia, gymnasia and
baths.

But the riches and ostentation of
the rulers led to an increase in the
use of a monumental scale in building for its own sake, and to the
increasingly decorative use of architectural forms that were structural
in origin. Columns were attached to
walls as ornaments and not as
weightbearers (round *engaged columns* and square *pilasters*). The
strict rules of the Classical orders
were weakened, and the highly
decorative, almost floral Corinthian

*The theatre at Epidaurus was
built about 350 B.C. by the
architect Polyclitus.*

*The sculptured columns
(caryatids) of the Erectheum
on the Acropolis were
built in the 5th century B.C.*

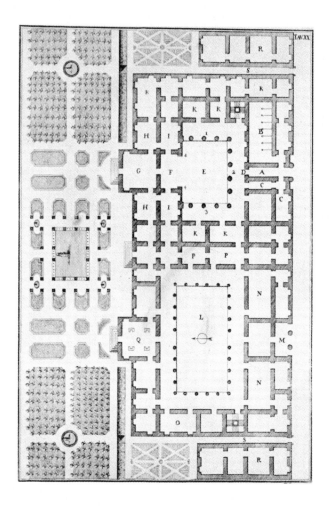

*The plan of a Hellenistic villa,
reconstructed in Galiani's 1790 edition
of Vitruvius. A entrance, B stable,
C porter's lodge, D gate, E and L
courtyards with 1, 2, 3 arcades, and
4, 5 pilasters, F atrium, G and Q rooms,
H bedrooms, I lavatories, K triclinium
M porch, N triclinium and picture gallery,
O library, P reception rooms, R guest
houses, S corridors.*

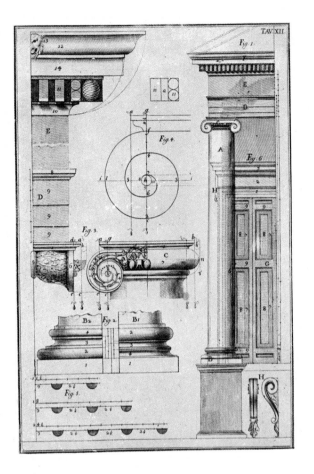

Order had its heyday. Only one structural development of any importance took place, and that was the use of the arch, perhaps as a result of contact with Mesopotamian builders. It consisted of a series of stone wedges fitted together over semicircular wooden casework which could then be removed, leaving the stones firmly in place. In the hands of the Romans, who at this time were establishing their hold over the Italian peninsula, this development was to make possible some of the most impressive engineering in the ancient world.

This final stage, when the creative impulses of Greek art and civilization had their most spectacular expression, is called "Hellenistic".

The Classical legacy

When the Romans absorbed the outward forms of Greek civilization for their empire, it was the Hellenistic style in architecture that they made their own. After all, it was the sum of five hundred years of con-

This Italian translation by Galiani in 1790 of Vitruvius's architectural treatise, explained and illustrated the rules of the Ionic Order.

Fallen giant — one of the colossal figures that supported the frieze of the temple of Olympian Zeus at Agrigentum on Sicily.

The 15th-century B.C. Doric temple of Concord at Agrigentum.

tinuous achievement. So, when the artists and architects of the Italian Renaissance rediscovered the qualities of Classical art in the 15th century A.D. they saw it at first through a Roman-Hellenistic perspective. They accepted a whole package of "style", applying its "rules" with enthusiasm before they understood the historical evolution that lay behind it. Thus there arose that obsession with the Classical Orders, as if they were in themselves the key to good architecture, that dominated the Renaissance and Baroque periods and reached a peak with the 18th and 19th century cult of neo-Classicism.

Doric temples at Paestum – the so-called basilica in the foreground is the oldest of the three beautifully preserved Greek temples there. The 5th century temple of Poseidon is in the background.

CHAPTER 7

ENGINEERING AND
IMPERIALISM

The Roman way of life, with its authoritarian discipline, its colonization and its materialism, has never been less admired than it is today. Nothing Roman can be found on my student friend's montage, although the generations before him would very likely have cut out a picture of the Pont du Gard, that majestic aqueduct which used to seem a symbol of the strength and practical nature of Roman civilization—entirely structural, free from superfluous ornament, peaceful in its purpose and incredibly durable.

From a cattle market (*forum* in Latin) in a damp little valley between two hills called Palatine and Capitol, living under the overlordship of the Etruscans, the Roman state robbed, bullied and plundered its way through three centuries to become the greatest politically unifying influence in the history of Europe. The practical nature of this success story was due to something hard and pragmatic in the Roman character. Its positive side is seen in its engineering achievements, for that is what Roman architecture really is.

Above left: The Pont du Gard in southern France was built in the 1st century A.D. and is one of the finest examples of Roman engineering.

Left: The remains of Ostia, the port of ancient Rome, have been excavated over the last century.

New types of buildings

The needs of the Romans for buildings, both in the capital city itself and in the many administrative centres throughout the empire, were much greater than those of the compact city states of the Greek world. The building of granaries, cisterns, aqueducts, law courts, baths and theatres demanded more flexibility in the handling of interior spaces than was possible by the strict application of Classical Greek forms of architecture. So the Romans were lucky that they inherited the Etruscan's skills in earthworks and masonry, while also being able to draw on the experienced refinement of the Greek architects from the cities of southern Italy and Sicily, when they came under the sway of the Roman Republic.

A natural advantage enjoyed by the Roman builders was that, having discovered the potentialities of concrete as a structural material, they were able, thanks to the presence of fine volcanic gravels in southern Italy, to develop an improved, lightweight *cementum*. This material, easy to handle, would set hard within its sheath of bricks in the form of arches, vaults and domes, on a scale impossible to achieve using traditional stone masonry. The Roman mastery of stone, brick and concrete, and the consequent engineer-

The Roman Composite capital which was made up of Ionic and Corinthian features.

Julia Domna, the wife of the emperor Septimius Serverus, is represented as a priestess of Isis, the Egyptian goddess, in this 2nd-century A.D. statue.

The arcading of the Roman amphitheatre built by the emperor Titus in 79 A.D. and known as the Colosseum. It illustrates particularly well the Roman use of rounded forms.

ing advances they made in handling ever larger spaces were allied to the expansion of Roman rule throughout the Mediterranean area and beyond. Public works of a standardized pattern imposed the Roman way of life on many cultures, but it was a way of life which brought all its subject nations into the mainstream of a universal civilization.

No compromise

The Roman stamp was everywhere throughout the empire, and although it lacked refinement and imagination and used the forms of Classical art weakly as a mere surface decoration, it insured the improvement of city life and the rule of law. Different religions were tolerated so long as the local cults could be brought neatly and quietly within the fairly undemanding framework of the Roman state religion. Quaint new temples could easily be designed to suit their special ceremonies, and given a normal coating of Corinthian pilasters. But trouble came when Roman rule found itself faced by believers whose faith was so strong that they were not prepared to "fit in" on an equal footing with other religions. Here, no civilized compromise was possible. There was head-on collision with all that the Romans stood for: the Temple of Jerusalem was totally destroyed by the Romans, and the public places of the Empire ran with the blood of recalcitrant Christians, but for the past fifteen hundred years there has been no Roman Empire, only ruins.

Roman remains

Even after fifteen hundred years, however, many Roman ruins—especially those with oval, semicircular or circular plans, the circuses, theatres and rotundas which the Roman architects developed so successfully—remain breathtakingly impressive. The concrete dome of the Pantheon in Rome had the largest diameter (142 feet 9 inches) of any dome that had ever been built, or was to be built until the Renaissance.

The homes of the well-to-do, as we can see from the houses and villas excavated at Pompeii and Herculaneum, were spaciously laid out and well organized, but not significantly different from similar houses in Greek cities anywhere in the Mediterranean. In the countryside, Roman landowners built themselves houses of a similar layout, but with the addition of farm buildings. These were the *villas* found in all those parts of Europe, North Africa and the Near East where the empire was established long enough for Romanization to permeate.

In the cities, Roman engineering made possible a high-density population in tenement buildings called *insulae*, rising to as many as six storeys, with large spaces on each floor, subdivided among tenants by partitions made of mats or boards.

There is one other type of building which is uniquely Roman and which has made a lasting impression on the European imagination. This is the triumphal arch. A symbol more than a building, it derived from the custom of a communal celebration of the army and its general returning from a successful campaign. In a way it typifies Roman architecture, being in essence a sturdy city gate, prinked out with surface ornament borrowed from the Greeks. It is a symbol which has been frequently imitated, sometimes quite modestly, as in London's Marble Arch, and sometimes spectacularly, as in the Arc de Triomphe in Paris.

Since the Middle Ages the ancient Roman Theatre of Marcellus has been used as living accommodation.

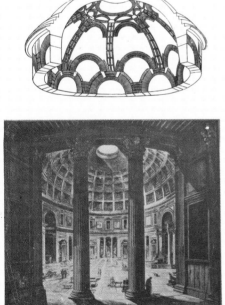

The Italian architect Piranesi drew up this plan of the dome of the Pantheon in Rome and painted a picture of the interior.

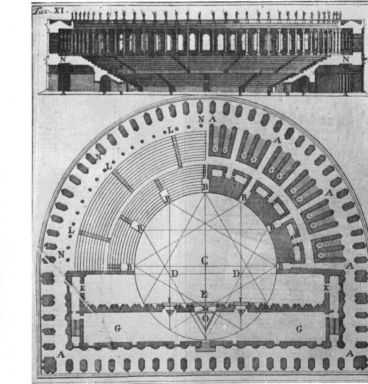

A Roman theatre according to Vitruvius — plan from Perrault's edition of 1674. A colonnade, B entrances, C orchestra, D proscenium, E stage, G vestibule, H and I "palace gate" and side entrances, K stage doors, L stairways, N gallery, O stage machinery.

Above: *Artist's impression of the Great Wall of China.*

Below: *A 20th-century wickerwork bridge over the River Min in China. This style of bridge has not changed over the centuries.*

CHAPTER 8

TRADITIONS OF ASIA

For most Westerners, awareness of architecture in the Far East is minimal. It is difficult for us to guess the age or period of a masterpiece of Indian, Chinese or Japanese architecture, and as we are not familiar with the history of their civilizations, what we see reproduced in pictures often seems confusing and elaborate.

Some modern Japanese architects are, of course, now known worldwide, and if a photograph of one of Kenzo Tange's buildings made its appearance among the pin-ups on the wall of that student's room, one would be forgiven for not recognizing at once that it was not in Europe or the United States. Perhaps it will soon be part of everyone's education to visit the homelands of the great civilizations and to see the Great Wall of China as naturally as one's own town hall. Until then, however, we must make do with photographs and films if we want to get an idea of how their great buildings look, and of the environment in which they are placed.

Origins

Archaeology gives us clues to the spread of essential human skills in pottery and the working of metals eastwards from Mesopotamia, across the Indus into India and through central Asia to northern China. In these regions, where Stone Age populations were already settled and evolving their own civilizations, the technical advances brought from Mesopotamia found favourable conditions for rapid development. An elaborate Bronze Age culture arose rapidly in the region of the Yangtze Kiang in China around 1500 B.C. while the Indus Valley civilization of India is known to have been flourishing in the third millenium B.C.

Europe at this time was evolving through the Stone Age. In fact, it is only in the last three or four hundred years, and especially in the last one hundred and fifty, that the technical accomplishment of Western civilization became so strong that it could dominate the whole of humanity. In looking at the architecture of India and the Far East, therefore, we must not use as our terms of reference our own Western civilization. It is rather like eating Chinese food for the first time—the ingredients are not so very different from what we know, but the treatment of them produces a very unfamiliar taste.

A new relationship

We are entering an era of new relationships with the peoples of Asia, an era precipitated by the forcing house of World War II. We

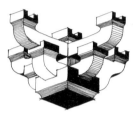

The bracket-cluster (tou-kung) — the Chinese capital — is a complicated wooden structure.

A 7th-century A.D. statuette of fired clay depicting a court lady of the Tang dynasty.

57

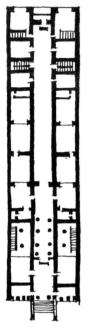

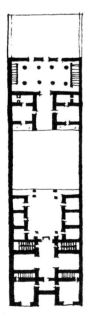

are being brought into even closer contact with each other as a result of military and political involvement in Asia, the penetration of Japanese manufactures into our own homelands, or natural and political disasters on the Indian subcontinent which catch the sympathy of the world.

Continuity in China

It is a surprising fact that despite the old appearance of many Chinese cities and temples, there are very few really ancient buildings in China. There are none as old as the Pantheon in Rome, and few even as old as our European Gothic cathedrals. Most of the oldest examples of Chinese architecture date from the Ming dynasty which covered the period from 1468 to 1644. What deceives the Western eye is the extraordinary continuity in the use of forms, materials and constructional methods from earlier times. Continuity and consistency are the strongest characteristics of Chinese architecture and planning. Each unit forms part of a larger whole, so that architecture and town planning tend to be larger or smaller expressions of the same principles.

Since prehistoric times, a Chinese house has consisted of a walled enclosure with a south-facing entrance, and this has been used until this century. The same rule, with minor variations, is applied everywhere, from the single dwelling to the vast, rectangular walled cities with their main gates in the centre of the south wall, a grid pattern layout of streets with the main street running from north to south.

Peking offers the best-known example of Chinese town planning on the grand scale. From A.D. 1403 to 1552 the city was rebuilt on its present site, with an extension to the

city walls to enclose new suburbs. The whole area (which includes a series of artificial lakes built by Kublai Khan) is laid out on a north-south axis, with the walled Imperial City in the centre and, within that, the walled Imperial Palace. Everything is linear, symmetrical and harmonious. All buildings, private and public, face south. And outside the original south gate (though now enclosed within a suburb) lies the perfectly rectilinear complex of the Temple and Altar of Heaven. The precinct and its buildings, built and coloured in the traditional Chinese manner, have a geometrical perfection reminiscent of the machine-finish of some modern scientific installations.

These principles of order, stability and regularity, which are expressed in Chinese building and planning practices and, indeed, throughout their art forms, are balanced by a very different approach to the design of gardens and landscapes.

The Chinese have developed the art of recreating, within the small scale of a garden, a satisfying illusion of nature in its untouched state—the emphasis is all on recapturing the essence of nature, and immense artistry goes into the invention of miniature scenery, with wayward streams and waterfalls, grotesque rocks and the cunningly suggested solitude of forest glade or mountain slope. This contrast of the wilderness with the good order of cities and the ideal harmony of society, is said to represent yet another form of Chinese continuity: the nature-mysticism of Taoism, handed down from a very primitive era of Chinese civilization.

China's Great Wall is in itself one of humanity's most stupendous feats of civil engineering and of building organization. Snaking across nearly two and a half thousand miles of

The Temple of Heaven in Peking was built in the 15th century.

the earth's surface, it is a monument to man the builder. The Great Wall also tells us something about the time-scale of Chinese history: the eleven years it took to build (and, even then, it was the consolidation and extension of earlier walls) coincided with Hannibal's campaigns in Italy from 221 to 207 B.C. It still stands, after its latest phase of repairs in the 16th century.

Isolation in Japan

Chinese influence on the architecture of Japan—and on its art and civilization generally—was powerful and fruitful during several periods of history. But since 1853, and particularly the period from 1946, the influence of Europe and America has been overwhelmingly strong. Nevertheless, on several occasions Japan has shut herself off from the outer world for long periods of time. The effects of these self-imposed isolations are apparent in Japanese

architecture and building methods —the barely changing repetition of homegrown forms tending towards greater simplicity as time passes and skills are perfected.

This artistic concentration produced works of art, especially in wood engraving, painting and architecture which, when they became known to the West, had a decisive influence on 20th-century art and design. One of the sources of the Art Nouveau design movement was

The Gatehouse of the Hall of Supreme Harmony in Peking was also built in the 15th century.

the Japanese coloured woodcut, so much admired in the 1880s and 1890s.

For the pioneer architects of the Modern movement, the clean, functional lines of Japanese timber-framed construction and the interior spaces that could be extended or subdivided at will by the movement of screens, were a potent inspiration.

The original model of a Japanese house was a thatched, rectangular cabin made of timber or bamboo, raised on stilts for easier building on hillsides and to allow the heavy

rainfall or floods to drain away. Houses of this form can still be seen in south-east Asia. The climate and the danger of earthquakes made forest products, like timber, paper, bark and bamboo, the main building materials until the recent introduction of reinforced concrete. Methods of securing and enclosing these wooden structures remained basically the same, century after century, until a fantastically high level of craftsmanship was achieved.

The Japanese ability to learn from abroad and, by the application of a painstaking and superb native craftsmanship, not only to equal and surpass the foreign model in quality, but also to turn it into something essentially Japanese, is seen again and again. The whole apparatus of Chinese civilization, already in full and splendid flower under the T'ang dynasty from A.D. 618 to 907, was imported into Japan together with the Buddhist religion which was adopted about A.D. 538.

Government, writing, art and public building were copied, absorbed and subtly changed. The Buddhist sects which found most favour were those which accommodated themselves to various aspects of the Japanese character. For example, the teachings of Zen Buddhism, which were introduced from China in the 12th century dur-

ing a period of military rule, suited the outlook and life-style of the austere rulers. The emphasis on simplicity in ritual, self-denial and meditation was in harmony with their outlook and found its architectural expression in unencumbered temple enclosures, the sober simplicity of little pavilions for the tea ceremony (which in a uniquely Japanese way makes a ritual out of complete informality) and the bare raked pebbles of a "sand garden".

Modernized Japan

In the 20th century, Japan's use of steel-framed and reinforced concrete construction, adopted from the West, has been turned to advantage in a region subject to severe earthquakes and typhoons. The ideals of the international Modern movement in architecture—especially those of Le Corbusier—have been studied and absorbed in Japan. But neither the technology nor the ideals have been merely imitated, they have been given back to the world in new kinds of structures and planning achievements.

Kenzo Tange's two national gymnasia for the 1964 Olympic Games in Tokyo amazed the world by being built on the principle of "tensile construction"—the roofs in snail-shell form and supported by a complex system of cables. Expo 70 at Osaka again displayed Tange's talents in the space-frame roof of the main concourse (an inspiration for designers of the central areas of new towns), as well as those of many other modernist Japanese architects in pavilions built for commercial companies and industries.

Fertility in India

Of the total population of the Indian subcontinent today—Pakistan and

The Japanese capital, or bracket-cluster, is made of wood.
An 8th-century statue in the Ninnaiji temple in Kyoto.

India together—only seventeen per cent lives in cities. In the U.S.A., sixty per cent of the population lives in cities. Yet the record of Indian civilization begins with great prehistoric cities—Harappa and Mohenjo-Daro in the Indus Valley, which flourished between 3000 and 1500 B.C.

The subcontinent is such a rich patchwork of influences, styles are so varied, and the past is so turbulent, that Indian architecture was little understood by Europeans until comparatively recently. At first, even the dating of major monuments presented problems to Western scholars, and the prehistoric cities of the Indus have been scientifically excavated only since the 1920s.

The tea ceremony is an old Japanese custom. This tea house in Oiso dates from the 17th century.

These cities had been completely forgotten, but what the archaeologists found were large and well-laid-out cities on a grid pattern, with buildings of brick and wood. The style of architecture, together with the scanty remains of carvings, seals and pottery, show that Sumeria must have been the source of many features of this civilization. The later Hindu culture seems to have inherited some of the features of the forgotten cities—for example, the ritual bathing tank at Mohenjo-Daro and the form of some of the gods and sacred animals on the seals—but in general, the brick-faced dwellings, citadels and priestly precincts entirely lacked the elaborately ornamental treatment of surfaces which is typical of all later Indian architecture.

The sudden end of the Indus Valley civilization is connected with invasions from the north. Probably the invaders were the Aryan tribes from central Asia, the direct ancestors of the Hindus. Though originally a nomadic people, they settled in the rich lands of what is now the Punjab and the lands along the Ganges. Their wooden architecture, none of which has survived, was carefully recorded in carved stone—especially in the rock-hewn caves whose carvings imitate the details of ordinary buildings. The earliest buildings to survive date from the period when Buddhism flourished in its Indian homeland, between the 3rd and the 1st centuries A.D. Stone was now the usual building material, and high skill in stone-working was shown in the large and elaborately sculpted caves which were used as Buddhist preaching halls or monasteries.

Indian builders and sculptors have ever since had an ambivalent attitude towards structures in stone. To Western eyes, the temples they built have an affinity with natural rock that has been carved and burrowed into, just as those temples which they hewed from the rock imitate in every detail the free-standing temples built of masonry. The complexity of Hindu architecture reached its height in the Khajuraho temples of the 13th century A.D. in southern India.

Influence and counter-influence

The influence of Hindu architecture and sculpture spread very widely in south-east Asia, and produced many masterpieces, like the famous temple complexes at Angkor Wat in Cambodia and at Borobadur in Java. India itself was revitalized as a result of the Greek influence in art which followed Alexander the

A maharajah's court at leisure—from an 18th-century miniature by the Indian artist Amar Chand.

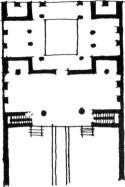

The ground plan of an Indian house.

The temple of Lakshmana at Khajuraho was built in the 13th century.

Great's march to the Indus in 320 B.C. The arrival of Moslem conquerors and immigrants from the 8th century A.D. onwards, brought a new direction to architecture over large areas in the centuries that followed. The link with the Islamic world, and especially with Iran, was dominant, but Moslem architecture absorbed many Indian features, both in decoration and structural form, reaching a height of splendour in the style of the Mughal period in the 16th and 17th centuries A.D.

The creative impulse in both Hindu and Moslem architecture seems to have died out in the 18th century, just at the time when the colonial powers of France and England began their fight for the domination of India. Under later British rule, care began to be taken of India's historic monuments, but architecturally the British raj has a meagre record. The two greatest building enterprises of the 20th century in India were both conceived by Europeans: the Viceroy's House at New Delhi by Sir Edwin Lutyens, and Chandigarh, the capital of Punjab, by Le Corbusier.

For the problems of today on the Indian subcontinent, of which an explosive population growth is the greatest and most immediate (the population is increasing by thirteen millions a year), traditional architecture offers no solutions. Neither the art of the stone temples, nor the airy structures of Mughal mosques and palaces, give any inspiration when the task is one of housing a popula- that is expected to reach one thousand million by the year 2000. We have seen the refugees of Bengal driven to building themselves shelters of sticks and straw, returning in that way to the earliest type of built human habitation. Only modern international methods of mass construction and prefabrication of buildings will be adequate if a start is to be made on resolving this problem which has reached such an appalling scale.

An early Indian pillar carving.

The Khmer culture, whose power lasted in Cambodia from the 9th to the 13th century, had its own distinctive art.

CHAPTER 9

AD MAIOREM
GLORIAM DEI

For nearly a thousand years, Christianity was the greatest, and at times the only, motive force behind the development of architecture in Europe. Even until the end of the first quarter of the 20th century, churches and their associated buildings formed an important part of architectural practice in the West. Today, church building commissions are still occasionally given, but for most architects they are simply one job among many.

On the student's pin-up wall, the only edifices sacred to the Christian religion which appear—that Gothic vault and that "vetoed" façade of St Peter's Rome—are there to illustrate an aesthetic point about form and function. This we can accept as representing the common view today.

Yet, if the urban planning and housing problems of our world have to be solved on assumptions which are very different from those which motivated the priests, monks and master-masons of the Christian cen-

turies, there is no doubt that the architectural history of those centuries has a relevance for modern architects. The story of Christian architecture is one of continuous development and adaptation, of structural discovery and architectural invention.

The first churches

The first interior spaces used by Christians for their own specific purposes were in hidden underground refuges—the catacombs are the architecture of persecution. Toleration, early in the 4th century, brought the Christians into the light of day, where they took as their temporary meeting houses the civic basilicas of the Roman towns. When, soon afterwards, Constantine made Christianity the state religion of the Roman Empire, the first specifically Christian places of worship could be built. Yet even so, the ground plan of the Roman basilica was still followed—a pillared nave with two aisles and a vaulted *apse*, or recess, at the far end where, in place of the Roman magistrate, a Christian bishop now sat.

Outwardly, early Christian architecture does not compare with the colonnaded splendour of Classical buildings. Churches were often makeshift, re-using materials taken from Classical temples when these

Under its leafy decoration the Byzantine capital has a strong geometrical form.

Byzantine mosaic of a Christian martyr in the church of Sant'Apollinare Nuovo in Ravenna.

Above left: *Artist's impression of the 5th-century church of St John at Ephesus, of which only ruins remain today.*

Left: *The 6th-century church of Hagia Sophia in Constantinople became a mosque after the Turks conquered Byzantium, and is now a museum.*

were proscribed, closed and demolished. The joy and the poetry was in the liturgy itself, and an appropriate architectural expression for it had yet to be found. The economic and political fabric of the Roman world was impoverished and breaking down, and something of the austerity and humility of the catacombs was brought into these new and unadorned churches.

Byzantium

The upsurge of ceremonial in Christian worship came from the Eastern Roman Empire, which survived the collapse of law and order in the Western Empire in the fifth century. This gave a new direction to the architecture of the Christian religion. The shape of the new churches was influenced by the processions, the thrones and the symbolism of the acts of worship.

The largest and most spectacular building of all was ordered by the emperor himself—Justinian—in the imperial capital of Constantinople. This was the cathedral of the Holy Wisdom (Hagia Sophia), built between 532 and 537. Hagia Sophia was the sum of countless innovations—its vaulted arches forming a system of *squinches*, or arches, and cupolas rising up to the crowning innovation of all, the daring central dome, 107 feet across. The dome, of flattened form, stands on a square base and is a synthesis of Roman vaulting and Iranian-Mesopotamian brick cupolas. Perhaps significantly, its architects, Anthemius and Isidorus, came from the east—from the province of Anatolia. Even today, the dome of Hagia Sophia gives the visitor the impression that it is floating over the space below.

Ravenna, a link

At this time, strangely enough, Ravenna, not Rome, was the most important city in Italy, and a cul-

Sant'Apollinaire in Classe in Ravenna was begun in 534 by Theodoric.

The tomb in Ravenna of Theodoric, king of the Goths.

tural link between east and west. Rome was in ruins and the provinces had crumbled in chaos, with barbarian kingdoms springing up here and there. Ravenna had become the seat of imperial Roman government at the beginning of the 5th century, and nowhere else in the west were such splendid buildings being erected.

The Goths ruled all Italy from Ravenna for some fifty years, and then, in the reign of Justinian, Ravenna came under Byzantine control. This was its greatest period of prosperity as a nerve-centre of Byzantine influence. Much building had been begun in Ravenna by the Gothic king, Theodoric the Great, who adhered to the Arian sect of Christianity. He died in 526, and his mausoleum is a powerful monument, consisting of a cylindrical storey on a decagonal base, capped by a dome which is carved out of a single enormous block, 35 feet across and weighing 470 tons. The basilicas of Sant' Apollinare Nuovo and Sant' Apollinare in Classe and the beautifully proportioned octagonal church of San Vitale were begun as Arian churches but later completed by the Byzantines, who decorated them within with masterpieces of mosaic art, and consecrated them as Catholic churches.

Although the power of the Eastern Empire gradually failed, the influence of Byzantine art spread to central and northern Europe. The recovery of civilization in the lands along the Rhine, following the foundation and later revival of a new Western Empire, owed much to Greek influence during the 10th century. The Venetians, the most open of all western Europeans in their time to influences from the Near East, created an architectural style which was peculiar to their republic alone. It combined northern elements with Byzantine-Oriental decorative features, of which the domes of St Mark's are perhaps the most obvious examples.

The widest expansion of Byzantine influence was into Russia. There, the adoption of the Eastern Orthodox form of Christianity brought with it a kind of church building and a system of decoration and religious symbolism which, when changed from stone into the wooden architecture and carving of the forest lands of the north-east, became a style that was uniquely Russian. So Russian, in fact, that it was a long time after the Renaissance before the Russian clergy and notables could bring themselves to accept the "new" pagan style of Classicism in their country.

Left: *An aerial photograph shows a little-known view of the domes of St Mark's in Venice.*

Above: *the domes and cupolas of St Basil's Cathedral in Moscow, completed in 1560, are strongly Byzantine in form.*

CHAPTER 10

BUILDING FOR A
NEW FAITH

The architecture of Islam is easily recognizable for certain common features and decorative conventions. In spite of local differences, the work of Moslem builders is identifiable whether it is in Spain or India, in Turkestan or Egypt. It is an interesting example of architectural forms and style being created to meet new needs. When the first wave of Arab conquerors spread out through the Near East and, with their armies of converts, into still more distant regions, they had no architecture of their own worth mentioning. It is true that building skills in the south Arabian kingdoms of Yemen in the times before Mohammed had made possible the construction of tall palaces of as many as twenty storeys, but this had little relevance to the problems of devising suitable buildings for carrying out the prayer rituals of Islam. The *caliphs*, or rulers, controlled a religious empire, and buildings were needed for the administration of justice according to the Koran and for the study of its teachings, as well as to house the caliph's court.

So, in the territories which they

Above left: *Artist's impression of the fortress-palace of Qasr al-Hayr in the Syrian desert.*

Left: *A desert nomad's tent at Midelt in Morocco.*

conquered from the Byzantines and the Sassanians, and converted to their new, puritanical faith, the Arabs took over and adapted the building and decorative techniques of both the Greek and Iranian cultures. The result was an architecture which is traceable to these sources, but has become totally distinct and Islamic.

From tents to mosques

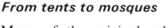

Many of the original soldiers of Islam must have been nomadic tribesmen whose idea of architecture may have been no more than a Bedouin tent. Most social acts and the worship of God took place under the open sky, so the original meeting places for Moslem prayer were open-air enclosures with a few very simple features added: a fountain for washing, a niche to show the direction of Mecca, the Holy City, and a high pulpit for the preacher.

Almost as soon as this type of building, known to us as a *mosque*, had become established, it acquired another feature which in some ways characterizes Moslem architecture as a whole. This was a slender tower, originally built into the wall of the mosque, with a platform at the top. Its purpose was to enable the call to prayer to be chanted out high above the whole community for all the faithful to hear. As many of the

Islamic capitals are richly decorated.

Turkish gravestones today still resemble those of earlier times.

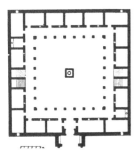

Plan of a Moorish house in Granada, Spain. As can be seen, the house was set out round an inner courtyard.

The Court of the Myrtles in the 14th-century Alhambra in Granada. The Alhambra is one of the finest examples of Moorish architecture.

prayer rituals were performed at home or wherever a Moslem might find himself at the moment of hearing the call, the function was rather similar to the angelus bell in Catholic countries. Probably, the idea was an adaption of Christian customs that the Arab found in Syria and elsewhere. This tower, called a *minaret*, had basically the same form in every mosque but varied in its profile and proportions according to the period or country in which it was built. The earliest ones were massive towers on a square plan, and this style later became typical of North Africa. In the hands of architects of later periods, in Egypt, and especially where Turkish or Iranian influence spread (as in India), the minarets became more and more slim and elegant. In the Moslem communities in Africa, nearer the equator, the outline of minarets often resembled an elongated native hut—a convenient shape when building with native materials like mud bricks.

Islamic style

Once the vocabulary of Islamic architecture had been worked out, and this happened quite quickly— in the first two centuries of the new faith, that is the 7th and 8th centuries —it proved flexible enough to meet all the needs of Moslem life and government. Religious colleges (*madrasas*), markets, tombs, audience halls and public baths could be built with a system of arcaded courtyards and vaulted or domed chambers. Inventiveness mostly went into a highly finished craftsmanship in decorative ceramics, stone inlays and stucco work, in all of which there appeared that delight in the elaboration and repetition of geometrical forms which is perhaps the most typical feature of Islamic art.

Two of the most famous examples of this tendency stand at opposite ends of the Moslem world: the Alhambra at Granada in Spain and the Taj Mahal at Agra in India. These two much-observed buildings are masterpieces of design and decoration, and sum up several important features of Islamic architecture. For example, we can see in them how there has been adaptation to a local culture (Mediterranean-European in one, Iranian-Hindu in the other) while keeping a distinctively stylistic unity which is Moslem and nothing else. There is also the subjecting of individual fantasy to an overall mathematical order. Under this discipline, fantasy flourishes in the details of decoration. In the treatment of lettering (calligraphy) as one of the principal decorative elements, we can see another Islamic speciality.

A particularly intricate kind of

three-dimensional, abstract decoration was developed by Moslem architects and craftsmen: the stalactite mouldings in the *soffit*, or underside, of arches or domes. This was elaborated from the multiple squinches built up to support domes over square, arcaded spaces. The first example of these stalactites are found in Moorish buildings in Spain, Iran and Turkestan (now Soviet Central Asia).

The conquest of Constantinople in 1453 led to one of the greatest Christian buildings in the world—the church of Hagia Sophia—becoming the chief mosque of the Turkish empire, thereby setting a model for the building of new mosques. In the city itself, the Sultans built the Bayezid (1497) and Suleiman (1557) mosques on a Byzantine plan. Similar mosques were built in different cities of the empire, such as Adrianople (now Edirne) in Turkey and Damascus.

Moslem cities

Private houses generally followed the traditional Middle-Eastern layout of courtyards enclosed by flat-roofed wings, usually windowless on the outer walls. The financial standing of the inhabitants was expressed by the materials used and by the size and number of courtyards rather than by any fundamental difference in building design. Towns as a whole, throughout the Moslem world, tended to be a huddled mass of dwellings, threaded by narrow and often roofed-over alleyways. An exception to this haphazard growth was the geometrical plan of the city of Baghdad, laid out by the Caliph al-Mansur in 762. It was circular, with four main gates, from which two main intersecting thoroughfares crossed the concentric rings of streets.

The mosque built by Suleiman the Magnificent in the 16th century at Damascus for pilgrims on their way to Mecca.

The 17th-century minaret at Shela, a Moslem village in Kenya.

CHAPTER 11

OLD AFRICA—
NEW NEEDS

Africa has the world's oldest great architecture. As well as having a venerable tradition of Christian church architecture that goes back fifteen hundred years, Africa has some of the finest cities laid out in Classical times. Yet, when we use the words "African architecture" we are probably thinking of a collection of mud rotundas, surrounded by a hedge of thorn. Why is architecture in Africa not the same thing as African architecture?

The lands north of the Sahara, bordering the sea, have always formed part of the Mediterranean world. Their civilization has shared, in turn, that of ancient Egypt, Greece and Rome, and, since the 8th century, of Islam. More recently, colonial rule from France, Italy and Britain has added its influence. Similarly, the eastern highlands of Ethiopia have belonged culturally to the Semitic and Christian world of Egypt and Arabia.

When we move south of the Sahara, into the real "black" Africa, we enter a different civilization. Basically agricultural, centred round the community of family and tribe, with developed arts, especially in

Above left: Mud-built mosque and huts outside Bamako in Mali, West Africa.

Left: Models of Togo huts in the Ethnology Museum, Berlin.

music and sculpture, black Africa has undergone the shock of assault from without by the advanced industrial nations of Europe, the consequences of which are still apparent in architecture.

Western building methods have been imported, followed by a white-inspired international idiom in architecture, neither of which has the slightest affinity with the roots of black African culture itself. The problem will not be resolved easily, but to support the form of civilization thrust upon them, the newly independent states of Africa must have their cities, their universities and their countrywide social services. And for all this, modern buildings are needed. That is the dilemma of architecture in Africa.

Ancient influences

At the time of the first European incursions in the 16th century, there were already large cities in the western parts of Africa, such as Timbuktu, Benin and Kano. Important trading and cultural centres, these cities owed much to contact with the Arab north. Archaeologists also hold that they may well owe something to contacts at a much earlier period with the ancient Egyptian civilization of the Nile Valley. Apart from certain Islamic influences, however, these cities were

An African capital from Hogon.

A Baule carving of mother and child from the Ivory Coast.

Ghana, sees a fuller role in society for African architects in Africa since they must wield great influence as innovators and propagandists of a new way of life, rather than simply as professional planners.

Solutions that are right in Europe and North America may be disastrous in Africa. As urban centres of industry and population grow, African architects will have to find the most appropriate built environment for people who are unused to the isolation and anonymity of city life, and who normally live their lives in a far more closely knit, family framework than we know in the industrialized West.

But generalized solutions for Africa are dangerous. A huge area with several different climatic zones is involved, and the population itself comprises no less than six hundred distinct cultural groups, with an amazing diversity of languages and dialects. There are about forty different governments with almost every kind of political system represented among them.

built in an African idiom, using mud and timber. Under colonial rule, little attention was paid to this idiom, except occasionally in the use of indigenous decorative motifs, applied as "local colour" to Western-style buildings. It is to be feared that the situation is not so very different today, when eminent Western architects are invited to independent African states to design their parliament houses and universities in concrete and steel.

A role for architects

Professor Graham Wilton, speaking of the university of Kumasi in

A complete change

The progress of independent Africa is not likely to be either smooth or regular. A complete social and economic change is being brought about and what its architectural expression will be is something which we cannot yet predict. It is for the Africans themselves to find the answer—to take what they need from the advanced countries and reject what is inessential to them. In the power and creativity of native African sculpture (which must include the sculptural forms of mud-built huts) we can hopefully detect a traditional feeling for the handling of volumes which may help to establish a distinctively African architecture in the future.

Conical huts in
Nigeria.

*The characteristic
conical roofs of huts
in a village south
of Bobo Dioulasso
in the Upper Volta.*

*Kenya has a modern
university at
Nairobi.*

A typical Maori house. The pitched roof forms a porch at the front, supported by a carved central post. The plan is rectangular, with walls made of boards and rushes. The facing boards are ornately carved.

Houses in New Guinea, like these in the Papuan village at Port Moresby, are still built on piles.

The modern university at Port Moresby.

CHAPTER 12

OCEANIA—A LIVING
MUSEUM

For the architectural historian the main interest of Oceania is one of basic research. On that sprinkling of islands across the Pacific—enclosed by the land masses and highly developed civilizations of Asia, Australasia and America—he can still see and study types of buildings in their more or less original form, which, several thousand years ago, evolved into the standard Chinese and Japanese house. For the rest, the building achievements of the Papuans and Polynesians (the two principal races in occupation when European explorers and colonists penetrated the area in the 16th and 17th centuries) display traditional forms of timber-built, pitch-roofed and thatched dwellings, handed down without much change and found throughout the area as a result of long migrations across the ocean. Wood was also the medium of most sculpture, though stone was carved in some cases and stone tools were used. The most impressive stone figures are, of course, those on Easter Island, and their origin is one of the world's great archaeological puzzles.

Building in stone was otherwise unknown until the arrival of the Europeans, except in areas where more advanced south-east Asian peoples, such as the Malays, had made their influence felt. In the Caroline Islands group are the ruins of two great cities with stone-built foundations, Nan-Matol and Pot-Falat, which are thought to have originated in this way. There are the remains of massive walls, nearly thirty feet high and over twelve feet thick, constructed of cyclopean basalt and limestone blocks, that may have had to be brought there on rafts. There were also canals and harbour works. By the time the Portuguese arrived, at the beginning of the 16th century, Nan-Matol and Pot-Falat were already deserted.

A Melanesian carving on a supporting post from New Caledonia.

Outside influences

Western colonial architecture in Oceania has been limited on the whole to the usual utilitarian or missionary buildings that are found elsewhere in the tropics. This island world is today merely an air bridge between the booming, industrial worlds of the west coast of the United States, Japan, Australia and New Zealand. The future of architecture in the islands is likely to depend on events in one or other of these expanding countries. Perhaps when New Zealand architects come to make their contribution in this area, there will be a representative among them of the Maoris, to bring about a synthesis of Western and Oceanic traditions, for the Maoris are the same race as the peoples of Polynesia and Hawaii.

Polynesian war god carved in wood, from Hawaii.

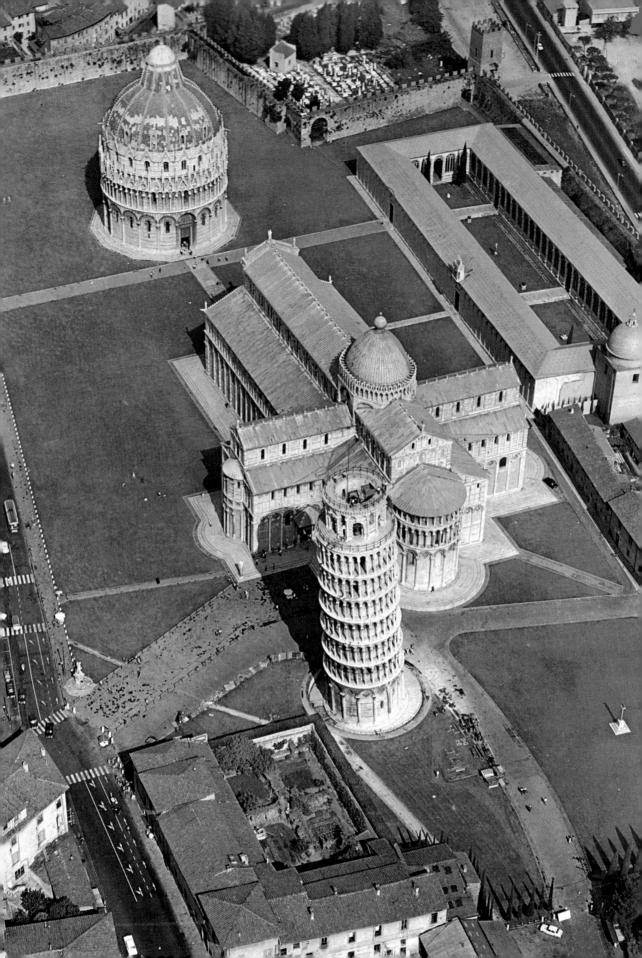

CHAPTER 13

EUROPE REBUILDS

We left Europe in the aftermath of the collapse of the Western half of the Roman Empire. We saw architectural influences from the Eastern Empire spreading from Constantinople and Ravenna into western, central and northern Europe where political chaos still prevailed. It is now time to take a look at these former provinces of Rome, as well as at the lands beyond the Rhine and Danube which had remained outside the Roman sphere.

The most important building activity was still that of churches—new churches in recently Christianized lands, and larger churches in the place of earlier ones. Basing ideas on the kind of buildings that were being put up in late Roman times, stonemasons and architect-monks in Spain, southern France and Italy developed a kind of building of specifically Christian inspiration. Round and octagonal buildings supporting a dome, usually richly decorated inside while bare on the exterior, were put up by Christian rulers; use was made of columns supporting a row of arches —a clear break from Classical precedents—and these various elements were developed into the kind of architecture known as *Romanesque.*

Aerial view of the cathedral precinct at Pisa showing, from top to bottom, the camposanto *(cemetery), baptistery,* cathedral and leaning tower.

Although in many ways the handling of details and the use of materials and proportions seem far less sophisticated than the standard products of Classical times, Romanesque architecture did in fact represent an important step forward from the technical point of view. For the first time, European buildings were constructed as a whole, every part having its function —supporting, buttressing and taking the load from each other— whereas the architecture of Greece and Rome had largely been a matter of arranging a series of autonomous, self-supporting elements—colonnades, halls, domed chambers—in a convenient layout.

The other model for church building was, of course, the apsed basilica, once the Roman court of law but now given a purely religious function. The use of arcading over the columns of the nave also represented a break from the Classical past.

Charlemagne

Two hundred and fifty years of invasions, migrations and turmoil had followed the collapse of the Western Empire before, in the year 800, a fresh start was made at establishing some kind of international order. Charles the Great (Charlemagne), king of the Franks, became Roman emperor in the

Romanesque capital

A detail from the dome of the cathedral of Santiago de Compostela.

West. He ruled over most of what is now France, Italy, Austria, Switzerland, West Germany, Belgium and Holland. At Aachen he built a permanent palace, with a chapel, modelled on San Vitale in Ravenna, which was also to be his mausoleum.

From this time civilization began to re-establish itself in Europe. Kings and bishops raised cathedrals, the religious orders founded monasteries and gave more time to teaching and to the copying of books. Trade developed and cities grew richer. Everywhere, there were commissions for artists—stone carvers, fresco painters, inlayers, goldsmiths and glassworkers. The establishment of larger kingdoms eliminated many of the destructive rivalries of local lordships and led to a more settled state of affairs for the agricultural and trading classes and the development of the feudal system, while the warlike energies of the nobility were at least curbed for a time.

The Romanesque cathedrals

The widespread gloom, provoked by forebodings at the approach of the seemingly fateful year 1000, was relieved when people saw the first of January come and go without the dissolution of the world about them. Christ had not come again in judgement, and the 11th century saw instead the rise of cathedrals and abbeys in the fully developed Romanesque style.

In the northern countries of Europe the basic feature of the Romanesque style was the rounded arch, but gradually different characteristics also contributed to the style. In Germany, as in Worms Cathedral, much use was made of towers and of small chapels off a semi-circular passageway, or *ambulatory*, leading around the main part of the church. In south-west France and parts of Spain—as in Santiago de Compostela in north-western Spain (begun in 1077)—domes were popular, then towards the end of the century in other parts of France and Spain, pointed tunnel-shaped vaults began to appear. This feature and that of the rib-vault mark the tentative beginnings of the Gothic style.

The 11th century church of the Trinity in Caen belongs to the Norman Romanesque style.

In France, besides the Norman churches like Jumièges, Bayeux and three at Caen, all built between 1037 and 1083, a church of immense importance was built in Burgundy, the Abbey of Cluny. This was the mother-house of the most influential branch of the Benedictine order.

Cluny's first church dated from 927, but by 1118 a third one had been finished on the same site. It was a vast building, 443 feet long, with five aisles and seven towers. It survived until the beginning of the last century, only to be demolished, all but for one transept which remains as a large church on its own. Modelled on the great mother-house of Cluny were several famous abbeys in Burgundy, including Paray-le-Monial and Vézelay, built at the beginning of the 12th century.

At one time the power of the Clunaic Benedictines almost rivalled that of popes and emperors. They were certainly among the most generous patrons of art in the early Middle Ages. They were also great promoters of pilgrimages, especially to the tomb of St James the Apostle at Santiago de Compostela. This encouraged the building of many fine churches along the route.

The travelling groups of master-masons with their artisans were another mobile feature of the age—camping, perhaps for a year at a time, at one site before moving on to a new commission. From Rome came the Cosmati "tribe", skilled craftsmen in the inlay of precious stones. From Lombardy came the Comacene masons. In this way new ideas and techniques were passed from one end of the continent to the other. The names of the architects themselves began to be recorded, such as Buschetto at Pisa and Paul of Caen at St Albans.

The fully developed Romanesque, massive in construction, expressive of the religious ideals—especially the monastic ideals—of the clients for whom it was built, was by the end of the 11th century reaching towards new forms. Already arcades, galleries and clerestory windows were being carried ever higher above the nave, and these features combined with the experiments in vaulting to produce the architecture of the pointed arch.

Detail of the nave of St Genou (Indre) in France, built between 994 and 1066, showing the three-storey screen with columns supporting Romanesque arches and a blind arcade.

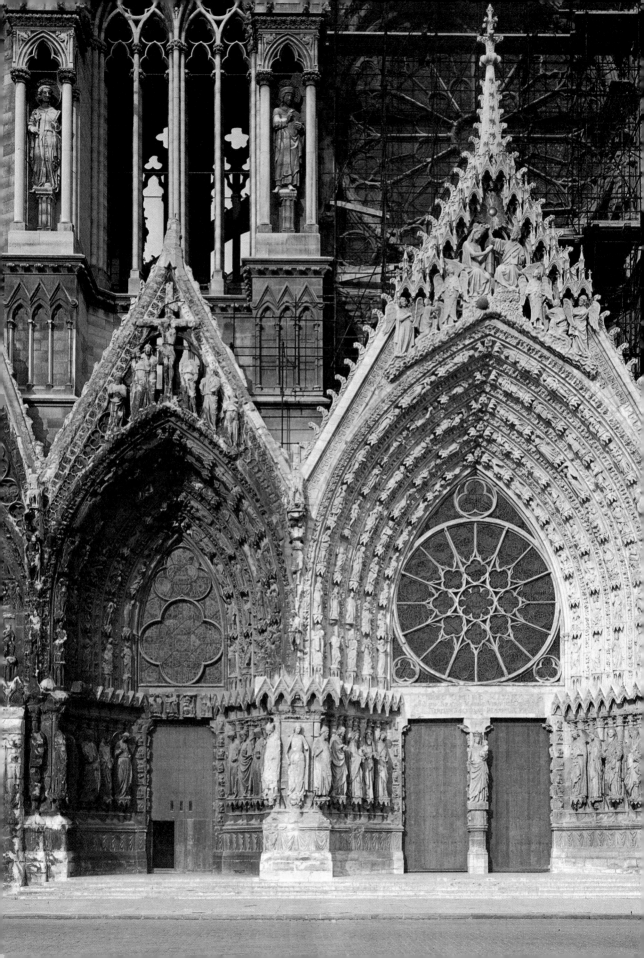

CHAPTER 14

THUMBS UP FOR GOTHIC

The student's bold affirmation of the structural and dynamic principles underlying Gothic architecture is shown on his pin-up wall. His "thumbs up" signal is implanted on a clever vertical photograph that explains without words what Gothic construction is all about.

Slim, weightbearing piers rise to a great height to support an intricate cross-vaulting that enables the building to be roofed in stone. The functions are clear, the architecture is an expression of these functions and, in consequence, a Gothic cathedral's meaning for a modern architect is very different from the romantic medievalism which it would have inspired a hundred years ago. The building whose photograph is on the student's wall is more akin to the Eiffel Tower's iron girders and the "okayed" pre-stressed concrete dome of Nervi's Palazzetto dello Sport, also pictured on the wall, than many so-called modern buildings that are piled up in our city centres.

More space, more light and more flexibility were the advantages brought to buildings by the new techniques of thinner, non-weightbearing walls and external (*flying*) *buttresses* to distribute the thrust of the main weightbearing piers. Large openings could be left for filling with decorative stone tracery and stained glass. In terms of height and airiness, the master-builders were ambitious and successful, but many problems of span remained unsolved until the Renaissance.

The Gothic capital.

The origin of "Gothic"

Gothic is a term that was invented by theorists of the Renaissance to describe the whole of the medieval art which they repudiated. At that time, in the excitement of rediscovering Europe's heritage of Classical art and architecture, all that had happened since the collapse of the Roman Empire seemed barbarous and inharmonious. The memory of the Germanic invaders and rulers who had supplanted the Romans in the 5th, 6th and 7th centuries, led the Italians of the 16th century to attach the well-remembered name of the Goths to the old and now despised style of the Middle Ages. In actual fact, the 6th-century Gothic kings at Ravenna had been only too eager to build in as Roman a manner as was possible at the time!

Vaults and arches

The gradual transition from Romanesque to Gothic began about 1090,

The 13th-century portal on the west front of Rheims Cathedral, showing restoration work carried out after World War I damage.

Detail from the Rheims Cathedral portal—a typical Gothic sculpture.

when solutions were found to the problems of vaulting. This involved the complex crossing over of rib-vaulting, and suggested the function of pointed arches formed from intersecting round arches. Whether this happened earlier in Lombardy, or in the Anglo-Norman realm, is not yet known with certainty. The earliest example of a large-scale use of rib-vaulting is in Durham Cathedral (started in 1093). The pointed arch made its appearance within the next thirty years and cathedrals were built in northern France which showed the use of these new structural features, making them what we would now call Gothic architecture. The first pure Gothic construction, however, where the rib-vaulting, the pointed arch and the flying buttress all came together to make an integrated whole, was the choir of the Abbey of St Denis in Paris, commissioned by Abbot Suger in 1140. Between 1140 and 1220 new cathedrals were begun on an ever-growing scale—Notre Dame in 1163, Chartres in 1196, Amiens in 1220.

In England, from about 1190, the first phase of Gothic is known as *Early English*, corresponding to *High Gothic* on the continent. Cathedrals such as Lincoln, begun in 1192, and Salisbury, begun in 1220, were based on French cathedrals but retained their own regional characteristics. In Germany and the Low Countries, Gothic was adopted from about 1250 onwards—Cologne Cathedral, started in 1248—and in Spain from about 1220—in particular Barcelona Cathedral (begun in 1293) which was influenced by the Franciscan church of St Catherine (1243) and whose features include a wide nave with no aisles and chapels built between the buttresses.

In Italy there was a long resistance to Gothic, and the truly Gothic style seems to have been largely a northern taste. Milan Cathedral was begun in 1385 with many masters and artisans from the north working on the construction. Gothic details were widely adopted in Italy for secular as well as religious buildings—especially in the rich and hybrid style favoured by the merchants of Venice—but technically they remained closer to Romanesque. Vaulting problems—and therefore the stimulus given to the development of pointed-arch structures—were avoided by the continued use of wooden roofs.

North and south

The step back to Classical forms was easier to make in Italy than elsewhere. When the first Renaissance building designs were being made in Florence about 1420, Gothic architecture was still being pushed to its limits in the peripheral kingdoms that bordered the Atlantic Ocean. In the late 13th and early 14th centuries, Early English had given way to adaptions of the *Late Gothic* on the continent. These adaptations were the *Decorated* style—characterized by intricate double or S-curved arches (*ogees*) and tracery on the windows, as found in Ely and Bristol Cathedrals —and the *Perpendicular* style— more in line with German Late Gothic and characterized by more functional stress on line rather than decoration. Examples are to be found in Gloucester Cathedral as well as in many parish churches and King's chapels such as King's College Chapel, Cambridge, built between 1446 and 1515. In Portugal, the ornate late Gothic *Manueline* style flourished at Belém and Tomar after 1500.

One decorative element of the northern Gothic style is a continuity in the feeling for coiled and tendril-like forms, which can be traced from the traditions of Bronze Age Celtic and Teutonic decoration right through the flamboyance of Gothic to Baroque and Rococo. The exuberance of Gothic decoration may reappear in later styles, but the reason that Gothic buildings ceased to be erected was that more convenient and more economical structures became possible as a result of the discoveries of Renaissance architects.

The Gothic revival

Nevertheless, two hundred years later, in England and France especially, Gothic architecture received a strange "kiss of life". A re-awaken-

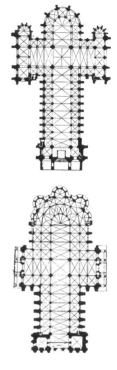

The cathedrals of Laon and Chartres in plan, showing the development of apsidical chapels and the wide central crossing.

Far left: *Flying buttresses on Chartres Cathedral. As in many French Gothic churches, the buttresses support the weight of the choir screen.*

The cross-rib-vaulting of the Chapel of the Annunciation in the Cathedral of St Just, Narbonne.

The early 16th-century cloister in the Convento dos Jeronymos at Belém near Lisbon, showing the Manueline style, a Portuguese variant of the Late Gothic.

The Ca d'Oro (house of gold), built in the 15th century, got its name from the mass of gilded decoration on its façade, and was the most beautiful Gothic building in Venice.

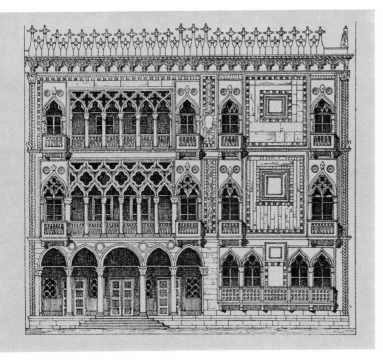

ing of interest in medieval architecture, and an understanding of and respect for its emotional qualities and structural achievements, appeared among men of culture in the first half of the 18th century.

To begin with this was a matter of a sentiment for the past. Then, from being the fashion of a minority, the revival became a serious, even a passionate issue. For some seventy years during the 19th century, Gothic motifs in architecture received approval in certain quarters as the only proper manner in which to build for either religious or social purposes.

At first, in the middle of the 18th century, the revival took the form of pointed windows and doors, and bits and pieces of tracery, often in stucco, used quite unhistorically to give a supposedly "medieval" face-lift to minor buildings like cottages and pavilions. Horace Walpole's "Gothick castle" of Strawberry Hill, Twickenham, finished in 1756, is one of the best known examples of this treatment. It is with the enthusiastic writings of Pugin in the 1830s and 40s that the full earnestness of the Gothic revival appears. Backed by the writings of John Ruskin, the English art critic and writer, and by a trend in the Church of England to return to medieval sources in matters of ritual, the movement gathered strength. Gothic was proclaimed the "only true Christian architecture".

There were other reasons why many 19th-century architects who were concerned about the state of architecture and society in their time chose to become "Goths". Tired as they were of the uninspired repetition of symmetrical Classical forms which often concealed the true function and structure of a building, they found in medieval architecture the freedom to design the constituent parts of a building

Augustus Pugin, the architect of the neo-Gothic Houses of Parliament in London, sketched this picture, showing his conception of the medieval town.

in such a way that the form expressed the function. A hall, a kitchen, a school, a clergy house, all grouped together or attached to a church, could be seen for what they were when designed by architects of the Gothic revival, instead of being squeezed into an abstract, geometrical plan and given a Classical façade that covered over the differences that lay behind it.

The seriousness of purpose in some did not prevent absurdities from being perpetrated by others. It was not during the tentative and sentimental beginnings of the Gothic revival that, for example, London's Tower Bridge was built, but from 1886 to 1894! And although the moral force of the Gothic revival movement had spent itself by the beginning of the 20th century, the style—like the latest work in the true, medieval Gothic before it— took many years to die out. The last major building to be built in the style inspired by Gothic is Giles Gilbert Scott's Liverpool Anglican Cathedral, begun in 1903 and still uncompleted.

At the Great Exhibition of 1851 in London, this floating model of a neo-Gothic church was shown.

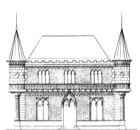

Design for a French neo-Gothic house drawn up in 1832.

Gothic and Classical features are evident in this design by R. Elsam in 1803 for an English country house.

CHAPTER 15

RETURN OF THE ROMANS

There is as little enthusiasm today for the revival of Classical architecture as there is for those Roman principles which once made a single empire of the European and Mediterranean world. The early years of the Renaissance and its initial achievements, on the other hand, still impress us because of the energy, artistic genius and evolving scientific thought which broke out, with such brilliant results, from the medieval pattern of life and thought.

The great advances towards rational behaviour and towards a human scale of values in art and social relationships—what we call "Humanism"—were made during that remarkable outburst of intellectual activity, the beginning of which is marked, in place and time, by the building of Brunelleschi's dome over the cathedral in Florence between 1420 and 1434.

The Renaissance

A concern for order, proportion and the uses of perspective led to an increased interest in mathematics, which in turn soon put into men's hands a new tool for probing the true nature of things. The inquisitiveness and inventiveness of

The dome of Florence Cathedral, built to Brunelleschi's winning design of 1434.

Leonardo da Vinci led the artist to design machines. Mathematics enabled Copernicus to demonstrate unpalatable truths about the nature of the universe. Brunelleschi, a goldsmith whose design won the competition for the dome of Florence Cathedral, was thought by his contemporaries to have personally discovered the rules of perspective drawing—a skill which added enormously to the abilities of all architects who came after him.

His dome was the largest since the completion of the dome over Hagia Sophia at Constantinople in 537, and the experts said it would never stay up, Brunelleschi's engineering calculations proved to be right, however, and his success places him first in the line of architects of the modern type. From now on, the architect in charge was no longer to be the senior of a band of master-builders but a professional man, a theorist, who designed, planned and directed the whole building and its construction.

The idea of the architect as superman, which has continued to the present day, was reinforced by another Florentine architect, Alberti, who not only designed some of the first buildings to get near to re-creating Roman architecture (for example the Malatesta temple in Rimini) but was also a scholar, musician, painter, scientist and

The Renaissance capital used antique features but never merely imitated.

Donatello's early Renaissance David, now in the Bargello Museum, Florence.

author of a treatise on architecture which put the designer on a pedestal.

In their enthusiasm for proportion and for reviving the Classical orders, early Renaissance architects sometimes put visual effects before comfort—as any visitor to the palaces of Florence can see. These massive and solemn houses, commissioned by members of the wealthy merchant class, express the character of these men who manoeuvred themselves into positions of political power. The porticos, looking like triumphal arches, were a statement of how they felt about themselves. The staircases are like stage sets for an opera and the room space is unevenly distributed. The reception rooms are so huge that they dwarf the residents, while the domestic rooms and offices are on a tiny, medieval scale.

The first steps in Renaissance architecture in Florence had been concerned with the treatment of façades. The buildings remained fundamentally medieval, with the revived Classical elements applied to the surface. While the more advanced architects, like Brunelleschi and Alberti, went on to develop a new and geometrical method of planning buildings, the new style spread to other cities in the north and south, in many cases still as a veneer on traditional buildings.

The small cloister in the 14–15th century Pavia Charterhouse, designed by Amadeo, is dominated by the typically Renaissance features of the Cathedral.

The winding staircase in the Belvedere Palace in the Vatican, designed in 1503 by Bramante.

The Renaissance Palazzo Vendramin Calergi in Venice, was completed in 1509 by Pietro Lombardo.

The Roman style

Enthusiasm for the revival of Roman architecture was, perhaps naturally, strongest in Rome itself. The popes, and the papal families, proved to be great patrons (as of Bramante and Michelangelo) and were also great retrievers of all buried Classical monuments and works of art on which they could lay their hands. The schemes of successive popes for piazzas, fountains, radial streets, steps and bridges made Rome, within a hundred years or so, the most imitated city in Europe. The grandeur of later northern capitals was largely modelled on papal Rome.

Palladio in England

The Venetian architect Andrea Palladio, whose cool and sober country houses in the hinterland of Venice set a new standard of domestic architecture for the rural retreats of the nobility, had a potent delayed-action effect in England, a hundred years after his death. Palladio was also the author of architectural treatises, and the publication of these in English early in the 18th century, together with the presence in England of Palladio's own drawings and of Inigo Jones's drawings of Palladio's buildings (made during a journey to Italy in 1613) fuelled the fashion for *Palladianism* in England from about 1720.

The same Palladian fashion spread to the then British colonies of America, becoming the basis of the later, widespread southern Colonial style. By that time, later in the 18th century, the airy Classical porticos of American mansions were to link up with the later revival of the pure Classical style in Europe—neo-Classicism—with the result that the official architecture of the new United States naturally took the form of that synthetic "republican" style, seen at its most attractive in Thomas Jefferson's University of Virginia and at its most grandiose in the Capitol building, Washington.

In 1450 Alberti was commissioned to convert a Gothic church into this memorial, the Tempio Malatestiano. The front was never completed.

The Basilica in Vicenza was an Early Renaissance palace remodelled by Palladio in 1549. The original building was enclosed by two storeys of arcades.

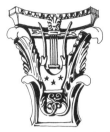

The "Empire" capital – the lyre is one of that style's most popular motifs.

The classical-style Hermitage in Leningrad was built between 1840 and 1882, to designs by Leo von Klenze, as a palace for the Tsar. It is now a museum and contains one of the greatest art collections in the world.

The Renaissance spreads

This uneven spread of Renaissance architecture had some curious results. While in the British Isles and America, Palladian Renaissance architecture was taken up at a time when in its land of origin it had already ceded to Baroque (which in turn had almost run its course), in another "fringe" country of Europe, Russia, it was the Baroque style, complete with French and Italian architects, that was imported as the modern kind of architecture.

Renaissance ideas made slow headway in central Europe and the Low Countries, and then more in terms of painting, sculpture and decoration than of architecture. Spanish architecture had remained Gothic, of a fantastically ornamented kind, until the end of the 15th century. Then, after 1493, with the reconquest of Granada, the last Moorish stronghold in Spain, and the discovery of an American empire, Spain became a world power and caught up with the new ideas in architecture. The first Renaissance palace was begun in Granada about 1540.

But it was in France that the Renaissance took firmest root out-side Italy, and where the most important developments were to take place.

The French king, Francis I, invited to his court at Fontainebleau a number of Italian artists including such outstanding figures as Leonardo da Vinci and Benvenuto Cellini. The architects Sansovino and Serlio stayed for a while and their presence helped the French to see that they could develop a native Renaissance style. Lescot and Phillibert de l'Orme were the first important architects of the new French School.

By the time that the spread of the revived Classical style in art and architecture was complete in all parts of Europe, changes had taken place in Italy itself. Michelangelo was the supreme figure of what is called the *High Renaissance,* but the parts of St Peter's, Rome, which were designed by him (about 1561–1564) are no longer truly Classical in spirit. A great creative genius has been at work, with the result that Classical orders and details are doing things they were never intended to do in Roman times, or in the writings of Alberti and Palladio. We shall come to these developments in Chapter 17 for they lead

to the Baroque and Rococo styles in due course. This is a good point, therefore, at which to look at what is meant by *neo-Classicism*, as distinct from the Classicism of the Renaissance.

Neo-Classicism

The baroque style never became really popular in the British Isles, with the result that Renaissance architecture—represented by Sir Christopher Wren, who died in 1723 —seems to run straight ahead and meet the Classical revivals of Georgain and Regency times, represented by the rebuilding of Bath from 1727 by the Adam brothers, the Nash terraces in London and the "Neo-Greek" of Edinburgh. In most European countries, on the other hand, the neo-Classicism that came to the fore about 1760 was a definite reaction against developments of the previous hundred years. It represented a wish to return to something more balanced and more seriously based on Greco-Roman precepts than what was regarded as the excesses and frivolity of Baroque and Rococo.

As this was shortly before the American and French revolutions, the revived Classical style began to stand for all sorts of things that had nothing whatever to do with architecture. In the mood of the time, it became a symbol for Republican principles on the old Roman model. For this reason, it seemed appropriate to the designers of the new Federal capital of Washington on the Potomac in the 1790s to build a neo-Classical city.

But it was Napoleon who gave momentum to the spread of neo-Classical architecture throughout Europe. The French took it with them to Italy and awakened in the Italians themselves a revived interest

in their Roman heritage. In Austria (the brothers Hansen), in Bavaria (van Klenze), in Prussia (Schinkel), in Spain, in Russia, architects looked to their Classical textbooks for correctness of proportion and detail, and to Paris for a lead in matters of interior decoration (the "Empire" style).

Only in England was neo-Classicism tinged with a lack of seriousness. When the Napoleonic Wars were ending and building activity could be resumed, John Nash ran up the visually effective backdrop of the Regent's Park development in London. His splendidly laid-out, speculative terraces were more picturesque than correct in their Classical details and thoroughly shoddy in their materials and construction. The theatrical element was even more pronounced when Nash worked for the Prince Regent in Brighton between 1815 and 1823. In Oriental vein, he changed a modest, Georgian country house into an exotic pleasure pavilion, encasing the neo-Classical core with gaudy domes, façades and minarets.

The Capitol in Washington D.C. in the United States, was begun in 1793 to designs by William Thornton, modified by Etienne Hallet and Benjamin Latrobe and finally completed in 1865.

OLD WAYS IN A
NEW WORLD

The pyramid of the sun at Teoti-huacán in the Valley of Mexico, photographed at night by floodlight, is another monument with a place of honour on our student's wall.

Europe, in the shape of Christopher Columbus, stumbled on a new continent when the real aim had been to increase trade with China and Japan. Once aware of what actually lay on the other side of the Atlantic, Europe bulldozed in with only three objects in mind: gold, slaves and power. The civilizations which were already flourishing there were smashed and the conquerors set about making their new empire as nearly like "back home"—in this case Spain and Portugal—as they possibly could. Their determination, ruthless and destructive though it was, has, we must admit, been rewarded by the development of a vigorous architectural tradition, combining both Spanish-Portuguese and ancient American tendencies, with a resulting strong character of its own. This vigour can be seen all the way from the first missionary churches and governors'

Left above: *Artist's impression of a Maya pyramid.*

Left: *The remains of Inca masonry at Kenko in Peru.*

houses of the conquerors down to the inventive modernism of Brasilia and Caracas today. The photographs on pages 96 and 97 demonstrate the continuity in the handling of materials and in the application of decorative detail from the pre-Columbian to the Spanish and Portuguese colonial buildings.

Before Columbus

As archaeology reveals more and more about the sequence and movement of its cultures, we can now say fairly reliably what had been happening on the American continent during the thousand years that preceded its discovery by Europe. We know that these pre-Columbian civilizations were based upon the discovery of the cultivation of maize, and that the two principal empires that the Spaniards found, the Aztec and Inca realms, had not been in existence for very long and were based on inherited civilizations built up by their many precursors.

But what really interests the architect is to know how these talented peoples, with no metals other than copper, silver and gold, solved the problems of building huge structures of stone and brick in regions affected by earth tremors, with results so impressive in their sense of exterior spatial composition and so geometrically exact in their planning and

A pre-Columbian carved column.

An Inca stone figure found in Tiahuanaco, Bolivia.

"Court of the Monks" at the Maya city of Uxmal in Guatemala. The remains of Mayan buildings can still be seen in many Mexican towns.

The "Temple of the Warriors" and colonnaded hall at the Maya city of Chichen Itzá in Mexico, built between the 11th and 13th centuries.

finish, that they now rank among great building achievements of world civilization. The temple complexes at Teotihuacán, what remains of a city of 50,000 people, and the Maya sites in Yucatan and Guatemala, the walls of Cuzco and the deserted city of Machu Picchu in the Andes, attract thousands of visitors every year from continents which their builders never suspected existed.

Tenochtitlán

The ancient Americans seem to have considered permanent buildings as suitable only for religious purposes. The homes of the peasants and the nobles were probably much the same as those to be seen in the mountains and forests of Latin America today. Unfortunately, the great Aztec city of Tenochtitlán, set on two islands in Lake Texcoco and joined to the mainland by a defended causeway, was utterly destroyed by Cortès in 1521 and rebuilt as what is now Mexico City. From the accounts of the Spaniards and of the Aztecs themselves, we know that Tenochtitlán was a fully developed urban settlement with the characteristics of a true city. It was rationally planned and astounded the conquerors with its size, population, sophistication and richness.

Above: *The late 18th-century church of São Francisco at Ouro Preto in Brazil was designed by the Brazilian architect Aleijadinho.*

Right: *Façade of the 17th-century church of San Francisco at La Paz in Bolivia, showing the richness of Spanish Colonial Baroque decoration, a style which can still be seen all over South America.*

Spanish church at Tiwa, Tiahuanaco, Bolivia.

A piano da baso

B pianta di sopra

CHAPTER 17

THE CURTAIN GOES UP

We have already noticed the unmistakable mark of rejection scored across the photograph of the façade of St Peter's Rome, among the pinups on the student's wall. This is partly an aesthetic judgement, for this part of St Peter's was never intended to be there and was an extension added by Maderna after Michelangelo's death. The top-heavy solemnity of Maderna's façade reflects the authority of the Catholic counter-Reformation which was then asserting itself.

At this period of European civilization—the *Baroque*—architecture had become sufficiently flexible for it to be used theatrically and as a means of propaganda. The patrons of Baroque were mainly bishops and rulers, and the ideas they wanted to promote were those of royal absolutism and of an unshaken, aggressive Catholicism.

Rome is the place where it all began. Michelangelo had died in 1564, and his very personal use of Classical forms in his great building schemes in Rome (St Peter's, the tomb of Pope Julius II) and in Florence (the Medici Chapel, the library of San Lorenzo) led his successors and imitators into further experiments. This pre-Baroque

This 17th-century design for a shrine in a Baroque church was never carried out (from a private collection in Rome).

phase is called *Mannerism*, and Italy is rich in buildings by Mannerist architects such as Vignola.

The Church and the Baroque

An important event at this time gave architects in Catholic Europe, and especially Rome, a motive for throwing their energies into the new dramatic style of the Baroque. This was the conclusion of the Council of Trent in 1563 which called for an art that would make the doctrines of the Church seem real and comprehensible. In 1568, Vignola began the Jesuit church of the Gesù in Rome and soon the new movement was in full swing. Sedateness, harmony and proportion were out and in their place came exhibitionism and the plunge into illusion and technical tricks.

The architect was now expected to be something of a magician and stage designer. The Classical orders were still to be used, but as in a game in which the cleverest permutation wins. Concealed lighting was used, stone and stucco, carving and painting, were merged to heighten the illusion, curved surfaces were emphasized and contrasted, as in the façade of Borromini's San Carlo alle Quattro Fontane in Rome. Squares and avenues were integrated with the general design for an effect of overall grandeur.

A Baroque capital on a pilaster.

Bernini's David *in the Borghese Gallery in Rome. This was one of the earliest works of the man who was to become one of the greatest Baroque sculptors.*

like Santa Susanna in Rome, stand in their own right. Borromini was perhaps the most ingenious architect of the Roman Baroque, using undulating lines, interplay of concave and convex surfaces and irregular spatial patterns. In Bernini, Roman Baroque probably found its greatest exponent. He was not only an architect (colonnades of St Peter's Square) but one of the great sculptors of his age.

From Rome this drama in stone, plaster and fresco spread and established itself throughout the Catholic world, local conditions producing their own recognizable style of Baroque. Louis XIV of France used it for his palace at Versailles. In Spain and the American colonies, the tradition of abundant surface decoration, going back to Moorish craftsmanship, produced an extravagant variety known as *Churrigueresque* (after the architect Churriguera). In Southern Germany and Austria a particularly light and frothy form was in fashion, with much fine wood carving and wall painting, the best examples being the joyous pilgrimage churches of

The dome of the church of San Lorenzo in Turin was designed in the 17th century by Guarini. Its eight-cornered star shape and Baroque style creates a strong contrast with the formerly sober architecture of Turin.

Carlo Maderna was Rome's first fully Baroque architect, and if his addition to St Peter's is deplored in comparison with the work of his predecessors there, his own churches,

Right: The little church of San Carlo alle Quattro Fontane in Rome, completed in 1642, was an early work of the great Italian Baroque architect, Borromini.

Far right: An example of the style which inspired Baroque— the 2nd-century A.D. Roman tomb at Petra in Jordan.

The pilgrimage church of Vierzehnheiligen in Bavaria was built in 1744 by Balthasar Neumann and is an outstanding example of Baroque architecture.

The Baroque nave of the cathedral at Passau in Bavaria with its stucco decoration was built by the Italian architect Carlone from 1680 to 1686.

Bavaria like Vierzehnheiligen and the Wies.

Chronologically, it might be possible to call St Paul's Cathedral in London England's greatest Baroque building, but owing to the time lag in the arrival of Renaissance architecture in the British Isles, it is not Baroque in the commonly accepted sense of the word, with its suggestion of dynamic tension, unbridled decoration and sense of drama.

Rococo

During the first quarter of the 18th century, a new style—even freer and more worldly—radiated from Paris, which had by then taken over from Rome the position as hub of all things new and fashionable. This was the *Rococo*, the name of which is derived from the French word *rocaille* for an exotic kind of seashell, the asymmetrical shapes of which have affinities with the free arabesques of Rococo decoration.

Above all a style for the applied and fine arts, Rococo appealed to the imagination of architects. They worked in it profusely, making the most of its emphasis on light, grace and a human scale. Although it called for a refinement of the designer's skills, it did not involve new structural methods or major changes in the handling of space. These were to be brought about by developments that took place during the early 19th century.

How Rococo got its name – the rocaille *shell.*

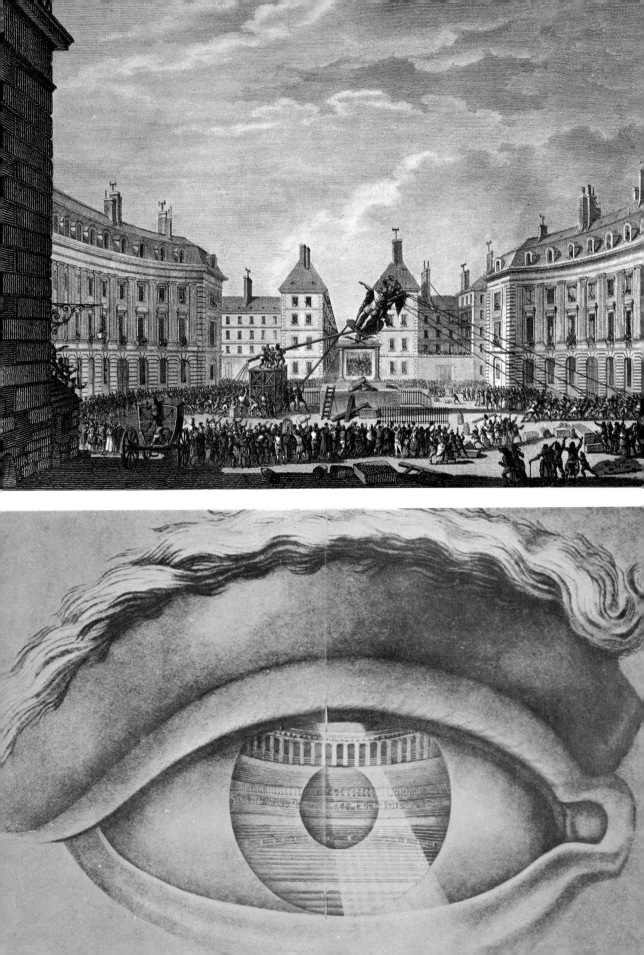

CHAPTER 18

THE MACHINE AGE

More buildings were put up on the face of the earth during the 19th century than during the whole previous course of human history. What are we to make now of the vast deposit of chaos, dirt, industrial sprawl, monumental imitations of the past, and hitherto unknown engineering structures which we have inherited from that prolific century? Some of the greatest advances in terms of both "user satisfaction" and of structural techniques were made, without which modern life would be far less comfortable than it is. At the same time, the greatest crimes of devastation and pollution were committed against our natural environment.

How does our student view the 19th century? What do the architectural pin-ups on his wall reveal about his attitude? We can see two frankly engineering structures: there is no problem in understanding why they have been chosen. The Eiffel Tower and a standard lighthouse exemplify the functional approach. They do not pretend to be anything else than what they are, and no "period" decorations have been added to disguise them. Then we

Above left: The old order falls—the overthrow of Louis XIV's statue in Paris in 1792.

Left: The vision of a new architecture— Ledoux's design for Besançon theatre in 1778.

notice the neo-Classical portico of a School of Art, taken over by revolutionary students. The cool, academic plinths and columns have been defaced—or is it humanized? —by posters, slogans and banners. It makes one wonder whether the students have rejected the architecture or have adapted it to their own purpose. At any rate, no other buildings from that incredibly productive century have found acceptance among the pictures on our student's wall.

The period can be said to begin with the eve of the French Revolution. Industrialism had already made its appearance, mainly in England and Scotland, while the political and social ideas of democracy were about to stand their first great test. In terms of art, there was an overlap between the serious and rather austere ideals of neo-Classicism and the new and exciting fashion of Romanticism, with its enthusiasm for great causes and its sympathy for the life and art of the Middle Ages.

Self-expression

For architecture, this meant that for the first time in history the clearly defined stylistic framework within which all architects, artists and craftsmen could work and know just where they stood, dropped

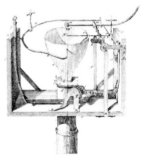

An English water closet, illustrated by F. Milizia in a theoretical work on architecture, published in 1823.

This design for a spiral staircase was devised by the revolutionary architect Boullée in 1784.

Mid-19th-century water pump which supplied the settlers in the arid North American prairie with water from underground.

The Crystal Palace in its original form in Hyde Park. Designed by Sir Joseph Paxton, it marked a turning point in architecture because of its materials – glass and iron – and its use of prefabricated building methods.

away. In its place came the more exacting and risky guide of self-expression, and a succession of revivals of past styles or imitations of exotic styles, accompanied by bitter arguments about their value and fitness for all sorts of uses.

Engineers and architects still tended to go their separate ways, but some of the railway bridges and termini are, without doubt, great architecture, while even such ardent Gothic revivalists as Viollet-le-Duc deigned to propose the use of cast-iron ribs and columns.

The architect of today probably looks at the 19th century with a mixture of admiration for the daring and ingenuity with which so much progress in building was made, and exasperation at the long delay in seizing the opportunities inherent in the new materials to create a new architecture for the modern world.

Idealism

Idealistic architects at the end of the 18th century, like the Frenchmen Boullée and Ledoux, inspired by the principles of the French Revolution, hovered between symbolism and functionalism in their vast, geometrical schemes for a new age of liberty, equality and fraternity. The logic was there, but not the practical sense. In England, where the Industrial Revolution was farthest advanced, and already showing its dire social consequences, an important step towards a rational architecture was made with the erection of the Crystal Palace in 1851. In its use of iron and glass prefabricated components, and its functional yet expressive design, it foreshadowed many later developments, but remained, at the time, a breakthrough that was not followed up.

The relevance of architecture to the social evils of the time was well understood by many architects. Some, under the influence of William Morris, the medievalist designer and

The first steam locomotives were popular subjects for lampoons in the 19th century.

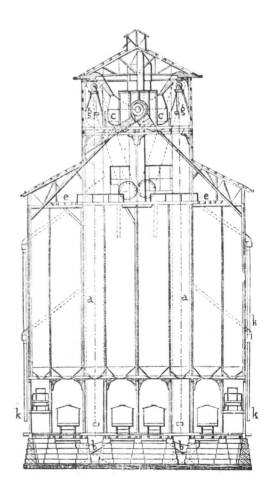

Vertical section of an American mechanical silo of the late 19th century.

thinker, saw the solution in a return to semi-rural communities of contented craftsmen, drawing on medieval models. Others looked to the more rigidly logical ideas of the pioneer socialist Fourier, who called for Utopian building complexes. He proposed that the old people should be housed on the ground floor, the children on the next and the adults on the top floor. There would be a centre for quiet social activities, including a library, a studio and a communal dining room, centred round a control tower with semaphore, pigeon post, a belfry, an observatory and a winter garden. Noisy activities were to be confined to one wing, with a ballroom and public rooms in another wing.

In France, Fourier's schemes remained on paper, but in the United States about forty communities were founded between 1840 and 1850 in accordance with his theories. The best known of these was Brook Farm at West Roxbury, Massachusetts, which lasted from 1841 to 1847. Unfortunately its architectural expression was very short-lived: the central building burned down

The Eiffel tower, built in 1888–9, was for a long time the outstanding example of iron architecture and is now the symbol of Paris.

The Palace of Electricity at the Paris Exposition Universelle in 1900.

on the night the members of the community were celebrating its completion, heralding the rapid dissolution of a brave experiment.

Skyscrapers

The United States' contribution to the development of a rational architecture for the 20th century took shape during the last two decades of the 19th century, when the first "skyscraper age" began in Chicago and the east. Until then, American energies had been mainly taken up with the solution of engineering problems encountered in opening up their enormous country—the building of railroads, bridges, dams and silos.

As the business sections of American cities became more crowded, the shortage of office space presented architects with the challenge of increasing the number of available floors on expensive sites. The electric elevator (introduced in New York in 1859 and constantly improving) made height possible, while better steel girders and a growing understanding of the structural properties of the steel frame allowed buildings to expand upwards to unprecedented heights.

The preliminary development of tall buildings in New York was quickly followed up in the rebuilding of Chicago after the fire of 1871. Chicago was then becoming the centre of the first truly innovatory American architecture, much influenced by the functionalism in the works of Henry Hobson Richardson in the early 1880s. In 1879, the man who was to become the "old master" of the American skyscraper started work in Chicago: Louis H. Sullivan, the designer of such later masterpieces as the Auditorium Building in Chicago, finished in 1889, the Guaranty Building in Buffalo, New

York State (1895) and the Gage Building, New York (1899). In 1887, a young mid-westerner joined Sullivan's office and so established continuity between the "Chicago school" and 20th-century architecture. His name was Frank Lloyd Wright.

New choices

The new technical possibilities offered by the use of iron, steel and glass were being seized by architects all over the world. Lighter and larger roofs could be built over exhibition halls, shopping galleries and similar public spaces. The introduction of electric lighting, from the 1880s onwards, meant less reliance on old-fashioned light-wells and a new freedom in the designing of large interior spaces. By the end of the century, it was obvious that science and technology were in the process of creating a previously unknown range of choices for architects and builders. As Paris displayed these new wonders to the public at the international exposition in 1900, the question was, would there be a new architecture appropriate to the opportunities of the dawning 20th century and, if so, what would it be like?

The East River suspension bridge in New York was built by J. A. Roebling in 1870.

The last universal style – in the late 19th century the San Carlos Gallery in Santiago, Chile, was built in the fashionable European style.

RUE — MODERN-STYLE.

CHAPTER 19

FREEDOM BREAKS OUT

The roots of 20th-century architecture lie, like the roots of 19th-century architecture, in the final quarter of the century before. The influence of the Chicago architects of the 1880s and 1890s on the planning of large buildings has to be understood, as well as that of the arts and crafts architects in Britain.

But the obvious break with the past came with the movement in the decorative arts and architecture known as *Art Nouveau*. Inspired in the 1880s by Henri van de Velde, the Belgian architect, in his search for a new free architecture not based on any previous style, Art Nouveau conveniently introduces the 20th century and a period of radical change and innovation.

The design solutions of the architects influenced by Art Nouveau—Gaudi in Spain, Mackintosh in Scotland, Horta and Van de Velde in Belgium, Endell in Germany, Guimard in France—do not have much to say directly to today's architects, nor do Art Nouveau forms appeal except for their amusing period flavour. But Gaudi, Mackintosh and the rest were very considerable architects, and each in his different way had a far-reaching influence on the architects of the next generation.

A fantasy of Art Nouveau – Rue Moderne-Style, *a design for a street by A. Robida.*

Working in Barcelona, Gaudi remained something of a loner. Looking at his uncompleted church of the Holy Family (Sagrada Familia) one is tempted to call him the most genuinely Gothic architect to have worked in Europe since 1500, in spite of his using hardly any authentic Gothic details. Charles Rennie Mackintosh, the architect of the Glasgow School of Art, strongly influenced the Viennese *Secession* architects and was admired in Germany, too.

Art Nouveau was principally concerned with applied design rather than basic architectural structure. It became very popular purely as a new design style and found its way into magazines, advertising and the design of everyday domestic objects, throughout Europe and America. In the course of doing so, however, it was often handled by designers of inferior ability, and because of its very freedom, Art Nouveau themes turned up in all sorts of feeble, exaggerated or generally debased versions.

Decisive steps

The originality of Art Nouveau had begun to fade about 1910, but by that time it had done its work and had provided the most creative architects on the continent with a free and unrestrained idiom in which

A capital with Art Nouveau motifs.

A gold jewelled hairpin in the Art Nouveau style, made by René Lalique, a French goldsmith.

The Watts Sherman House at Newport, Rhode Island, was designed in 1874–5 by Henry Richardson.

The church of Sagrada Familia in Barcelona, intended originally to be a neo-Gothic building, was taken over by Gaudi in 1883 but never completed.

to break loose from the academic mimicry prevalent in the previous century.

In Vienna, Prague and Germany, energies were being released which led to decisive steps in the direction of a new architecture. Among the Viennese architects of the Secession movement in the arts, Adolf Loos stands out. In Germany, the *Werkbund* group was founded in 1907, embracing the progressive forces in architecture and industrial design which were to achieve so much by 1914.

The dynamic connection between Art Nouveau and modern architecture is exemplified by Van de Velde himself. By the late 1890s, he was one of the leading European interior decorators and furniture designers in the Art Nouveau style. He then became a leading figure in the *Werkbund* and fostered the movement's involvement with industrial design. As head of the Weimar school of arts and crafts it was he who nominated Walter Gropius as his successor, and it was Gropius who established the Weimar *Bauhaus* in 1919, thus becoming a founding father of the modern movement in architecture.

The Chicago School

In the United States during the last quarter of the 19th century, the Chicago architects were producing both private houses and commercial buildings with a definite character of their own. The American skyscraper was by now well established, and in the Chicago milieu an architectural force of a different kind was maturing in the person of Frank Lloyd Wright, who was already building his highly original "prairie houses" for wealthy clients around the turn of the century. About 1911, Europe discovered his work, and

An interior in Brussels designed by Victor Horta, the Belgian architect, in the 1890s.

Glasgow School of Art designed by Mackintosh in 1896 combines austere form with original decorative details.

The Empire State building in New York, until 1970 the tallest building in the world, was built in the early 1930s.

since then European architecture has been in debt to America in one way or another.

The Modern movement

In the years preceding World War I, the forces of innovation in European architecture were gathering strength. Reinforced concrete was used for the first time by Auguste Perret for apartment houses in Paris; Peter Behrens was an architect of factory buildings and a designer of products in Germany; while in the world of painting and sculpture, Picasso, Braque and Juan Gris had invented the startling technique of Cubism.

In 1914, the German Werkbund organized an exhibition of industrial architecture and design at Cologne, where important, purpose-built pavilions by younger architects like Gropius and Bruno Taut were seen. So the foundations were laid for the

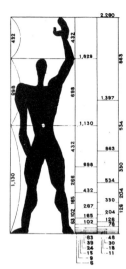

Above: *Le Corbusier's* Modulor *system of proportions for all architectural design (based on the human body) and his Villa Savoye, finished in 1931.*

Right: *Le Corbusier's pilgrimage chapel at Ronchamp in France was finished in 1954 and replaced one destroyed in World War II.*

Below: *An early sculpture by Picasso, which demonstrates the similarities between modern sculpture and architecture.*

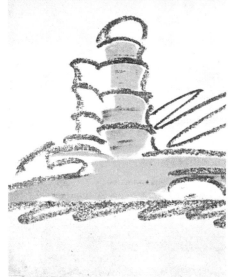

Far left: *In 1920
Erich Mendelsohn
drew up this
fantastic design.*
Left: *the design
brought to life in
1921 — the
Einstein Tower in
Potsdam, a typical
example of
Expressionist
architecture.*

new architecture of the 20th century, which was to take shape as soon as the holocaust of World War I had ended.

And at this moment, about 1920, we make contact with the architect of today. For from now on this is *his* architecture, the problems of design, construction and use are *his* problems. The question of the future of architecture in the next hundred years applies to *his* architecture.

Dominating the pin-ups on the student's wall we see the compelling face of the old master, Le Corbusier himself, radiating energy and persuasion on behalf of the new archi-

The airship hangar at Orly, built by
Freyssinet in 1916, has the functional
beauty of purpose-built buildings.

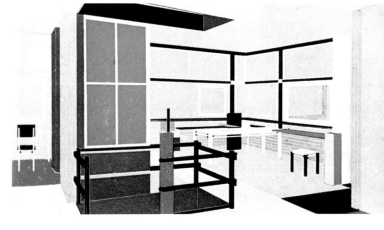

The Schroeder House at Utrecht was designed by the Dutch
De Stijl architect Gerrit Rietveld in 1924. The exterior (above
centre), and the interior drawn by Rietveld (above).

Walter Gropius and Adolf Meyer built this factory for the Werkbund exhibition in Cologne in 1914.

This fantastic design was devised by Hermann Finsterlin in 1924 – one of his unbuildable buildings.

tecture he believed in. In spite of all the developments in recent years, and certain shortcomings in Le Corbusier's ideas when applied in regions with different cultures and climates, he remains the superstar of modern rationalist architecture.

Other movements of the 1920s and 1930s which interest architects today are *Expressionism* in Germany, and the *De Stijl* group in Holland.

Expressionism and De Stijl

The Expressionists treated buildings almost like sculpture, using reinforced concrete because of its ability to support expressive shapes. They modelled exciting forms, like the "stalactites" in Hans Poelzig's Berlin theatre, the space-probing "observatory" of Erich Mendelsohn's Einstein Tower, the "oyster" of Hans Scharoun's Berlin Philharmonic Hall, and the "sails" of Jorn Utzon's Sydney Opera House. Some Expressionists preferred schemes which could exist only on the drawing board, like Hermann Finsterlin who designed unbuildable buildings! An expressionist line is found in the work of many living architects.

At the opposite pole stood the *De*

The interior of the Grosses Schauspielhaus in Berlin, remodelled by the Expressionist architect, Hans Poelzig, in 1919.

The Centennial Hall in Breslau, with its reinforced concrete dome, was built in 1910–13 by Max Berg.

Stijl designers. This was a group of Dutch designers and architects who were influenced by Cubism and who published their own magazine *De Stijl*. Their number included the painter Mondrian, and their cool, geometrical forms seem to have an affinity with abstract paintings. The small Schroeder House at Utrecht by Rietveld exemplifies their principles of clean lines, functional design and total rejection of any kind of ornamentation. The *De Stijl* discipline influenced architecture in many countries.

The Bauhaus

The focus for many developments was the Bauhaus at Weimar (moved later to Dessau), founded in 1919 by Gropius who held that all forms of

This model of Hurva Synagogue in Jerusalem, designed by Louis Kahn, brings to mind the architecture of ancient Egypt, by its use of solid form.

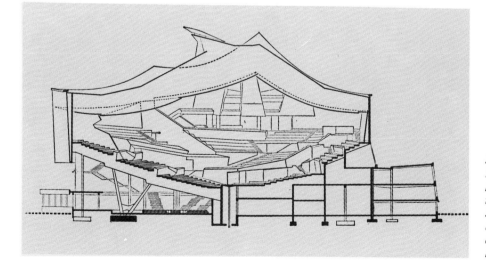

Section of the Berlin Philharmonic Hall, built in 1963 to a design by Hans Scharoun as a complex structure of rooms in the Expressionist style.

In 1920 Vladimir Tatlin made a wooden model of this design for a monument to the Third International movement.

A non-objective space structure by the Russian painter Kazimir Malevich, made in 1924.

Iofan's winning design for the building of the Palace of the Soviets, was carried out in 1931–33.

creative work are linked and interdependent in achieving a common purpose. The unity of the arts was his aim, and the teaching of painting, of machine design, of philosophy and of social science was all part of the Bauhaus course.

The ideals of the English arts and crafts movement of the previous century merged at the Bauhaus with the radical political beliefs of progressive artists of the 1920s. The staff and students of the Bauhaus stood for more than a system of teaching design—they stood for building a better society. They did not succeed in doing that, of course, but their writings, designs and widespread influence have left an indelible mark on the history of 20th-century civilization.

Constructivism in Russia

The Bauhaus was brought to an end by the Nazis in 1933, and in Soviet Russia the adventurous architects of the 1920s and early 1930s also fared badly. Advanced ideas had originally been identified with the 1917 revolution, and painters, stage designers and architects had worked together in the *Constructivist* movement with brilliant results. But the political tide turned against them, and architects and designers of the calibre of Tatlin, Malevich and Lissitzky were derided by the official propagandists. The Constructivists could do little for Soviet architecture, and official favour went to pompous and monumental schemes which have no interest at all for present-day architects.

Worldwide

Political pressures stifled architectural initiative in Russia and Germany, but at least the flight of refugees from the Nazis brought

one benefit to the rest of the world: it scattered the pioneers of the Modern movement across western Europe and America. Some came to Britain and helped to found the progressive MARS group; Gropius and Mies van der Rohe settled in the United States where they produced important buildings and influenced the work of many American architects after World War II. Frank Lloyd Wright, unperturbed, continued to produce a highly personal kind of modern architecture until his death in 1959. After 1945 the problems facing architects all over the world were more complex than they had ever been. Technology was changing, user requirements became more sophisticated, but the needs of the world's expanding and impoverished populations grew at a staggering rate. During the war methods had been developed for prefabricating houses and these helped to meet some of the most desperate human demands. The same techniques were later applied to the building of apartments, offices and factories from ready-made components. Called "industrialized building", constructional systems involving the installation of wall units, complete with windows and doors, helped to overcome the shortages of the post-war period.

The development of plastic in all its forms gave architects and builders a completely new material, while improvements in glass enabled them to design and construct glass-walled blocks that changed our ideas of what working in offices, schools and hospitals could be like.

Frank Lloyd Wright's house "Falling Water", built in 1936, is an expression of belief in a harmonious relationship between architecture and nature.

Below right: *the Palazzo del Lavoro in Turin, designed in 1960 by the Italian architect-engineer, Pier Luigi Nervi.*

Left: *The two-storey entrance hall to Tokyo City Hall, built in 1952–7. Its architect, Kenzo Tange, himself described it as the last work of his first phase.*

The Merz construction — a nonsense structure devised by Kurt Schwitters, the German Dadaist artist, in his own studio — represents anti-architecture.

Modern Expressionism — Utzon's Opera House in Sydney, begun in 1957.

CHAPTER 20

LIMITLESS
POSSIBILITIES

Building technology in the last decades of the 20th century has made almost everything possible. Provided that it can be designed and that there is the money to pay for it, we can now build anything.

Unfortunately, this does not mean that all architects are optimists or that the built environment will now be improved. On the contrary, architecture is suffering from as much confusion and doubt, for very much the same reasons, as all the other fields of creative activity.

The old, clear battlelines of the 1920s and 1930s have disappeared. In those days, the crusaders of a rational architecture, the followers of Le Corbusier, Gropius, Mies and the other heroes of the Modern movement in architecture, were lined up against the complacent defenders of traditional, imitative syles. Pouring scorn on their opponents, the men of the new architecture attacked and routed the enemy. But strangely enough, the aftermath of their victory looks like a gigantic architectural muddle. Most human beings are still living in sub-standard conditions, the homeless are increasing in number, the cities have turned into uncontrollable problems.

Architects are better informed, more highly trained, and have computer technology at their disposal, but their solutions to the world's housing problems do not seem to find favour even with the fortunate minority of Western countries which can enjoy them. Commercial clients order colossal office blocks equipped with every modern convenience, but the people who commute daily to work in them are not any happier. Factory buildings are hygienic and well designed, a far cry from the squalid mills and foundries of the 19th century, but pollution is such that the quality of their environment is not what it should be.

Much of this confusion and loss of amenity, in an age when we have the means—but not the will—to make the world a better place to live in, is reflected in the mosaic on the wall of that student's room from which we set out on this quick survey of world architecture, and to which we now return.

There is the longing for unspoilt nature, for the impenetrable woods —but the image of the forest is cut out in the shape of a Saturn rocket system pointing into farthest space. The dove, that gentle symbol of tranquil domestic life, has had a desperate plea for peace thrust into its beak. Various bizarre caricatures of spacecraft express uncertainty about the value of what we are doing up there on the moon. The unchecked urban sprawl of a great city raises an expression of disgust on a man's face, while at the same time a grandiose model of an

Tripod City – a project by the architects Courtois, Lajus, Sadirac and Salier of Brussels.

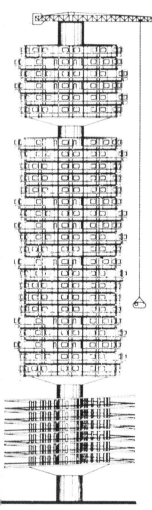

Unit Tower – a "plug-in" project for detachable capsules, designed by W. Clark in 1965.

architect-designed super-city on top of a mountain obviously raises so many questions that it is not an answer at all, but a whole new set of problems.

Trends

In this situation, what is there to say about the architecture of the present? First of all, we can see all the old trends at work, but not one of them being dominant, as used to be the case. There is Expressionism, the greatest monument to which is probably Sydney Opera House. The huge sail-like shells which form its roof and which are an outstanding engineering achievement, have added to the visual splendour of Sydney's harbour but architecturally they serve no purpose whatsoever.

There is Functionalism, seen less often in actual buildings than in impressive projects published in architectural magazines. The idea of capsules as living-spaces, to be moved around at will and plugged in to a "service core" for power, drainage and other necessities, is being explored by study groups all over the world. A logical development of the same idea is that even the capsules should be done away with. The creation of an artificial environment with warm-air screens and mobile plumbing and cooking facilities has been shown to be feasible by the British avant-garde group, Archigram.

There is Romanticism in the form of escapist encampments built of suburban débris by drop-out communes in the United States.

There is real social concern in the work done on various kinds of disaster housing for the victims of homelessness. Students and practising architects have designed pre-fabricated dwellings of plastic, metal, or even cardboard, that can be stored away until they are needed.

There is Monumentalism, intended to flatter the wealthy corporate client. Perhaps we do not get anything so bad as an Ancient Egyptian office building these days, but the business centres of our cities can show us many examples of fussy detail on a huge scale, and layouts, portals and roof-lines which serve no other purpose than to inflate the occupant's sense of importance.

Teamwork

Architecture is becoming more and more a matter of teamwork by specialists, while the client is more and more frequently a corporate body, such as a government authority, a commercial corporation or a

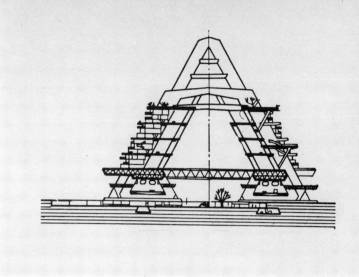

Experimental mobile housing units designed by J. Schein in 1967.

Section of a linear floating city designed by Tange and others in 1959.

university. Faced with a situation in which it is no longer possible for the architect to be a one-man master-builder, commanding all the skills and trades of the building process, designing, controlling and even furnishing the project, it is not surprising that architects all over the world are earnestly questioning themselves about their future role. Although it would not be easy to find an architect with a solution to the problems of our polluted, over-crowded, underhoused and under-fed world, probably at no other time in history have so many architects been working whose concern it was to make the world a better place for everyone to live.

Taking our last look at the pin-ups on the student's wall, we should perhaps notice the girl in the capsule and ask ourselves whether her cramped posture, in that carefully designed "environment", is really what we want from the architecture of the future. After all, we now know that everything is possible.

Hippy homes at Drop City, Colorado, in 1969.

ACKNOWLEDGMENTS

Endpapers by Fotoptica. G. Alzati: 22, 27, 29, 37, 42, 63, 71. *Architecture of Bridges* by Moch (1949): 56. P. M. Bardi: 8, 10, 11, 12, 13, 14, 15, 16, 17, 18, 19, 21, 22, 23, 24, 31, 34, 35, 38, 39, 41, 43, 45, 49, 50, 52, 55, 56, 59, 70, 72, 74, 76, 80, 81, 85, 86, 87, 90, 97, 98, 100, 101, 102, 103, 104, 105, 106, 107, 108, 110, 111, 112, 113, 114, 115, 116, 117, 118, 120, 121. C. Bevilacqua: 34, 35, 36, 40, 42, 43, 46, 47, 48, 49, 51, 63, 64, 73, 82, 88, 91, 99. G. Bonora: 6. Caramico: 16. C.E.A: 13. *Design Quarterly* (1965): 120. *De Stijl,* Stedelijk Museum (1951): 113. Edition Studio: 85. Farabola: 84. A. Feininger: 10. N. Gaudenzi: 26, 29, 60, 75, 95, 97. *Japanese Architecture and Gardens* by O. Hirotaro (1969): 60. *Kishangarh Painting* by Dickinson & Khandalavala (1959): 62. B. Kossoy: 24. G. Mairani: 20, 31, 38, 45, 55, 67, 68, 70, 76, 79, 81, 83, 92, 118. Marzari: 80. Moncalvo: 117. Ostuni: 28, 71. G. Pagano: 30. Preti: 14, 111. *Progressive Architecture* (1966): 18. Rizzoli Editore: 78. Scala: 54. S.E.F: 23, 25, 28, 30, 32, 33, 36, 44, 50, 51, 52, 53, 57, 58, 59, 61, 65, 66, 67, 69, 72, 75, 80, 86, 89, 90, 91, 93, 94, 96, 97, 100, 101, 110. Titus: 20. University of Philadelphia Expedition: 39. Drawings by S. Coradeschi.

FURTHER READING

Ackermann, J. S. and Carpenter, R. *Art and Archaeology* Prentice-Hall 1963 (U.K. and U.S.)

Burchard, J. and Brown, A. B. *The Architecture of America* Gollanz 1966 (U.K.), Atlantic Monthly Press 1961 (U.S.)

Clark, K. *The Gothic Revival* Penguin Books 1964 (U.K. and U.S.)

Hinton, D. *Architecture and Town Planning* Advisory Centre for Education 1968 (U.K.)

Hurlimann, M. and Meyer, P. *English Cathedrals* Thames and Hudson 1950 (U.K.)

Kauffmann, E. *Architecture in the Age of Reason* Dover Publications 1955 (U.K.)

Kidson, P. and Murray, P. *History of English Architecture* Penguin Books 1965 (U.K. and U.S.)

Kubler, G. and Soria, M. *Art and Architecture in Spain and Portugal and their American Dominions 1500-1800* Pelican History of Art 1959 (U.K. and U.S.)

Le Corbusier, C.-E. J. *Towards a New Architecture* The Architectural Press 1970 (U.K.), Praeger 1959 (U.S.)

Moholy-Nagy, L. *New Vision* Wittenborn 1964 (U.S.)

Moore, L. *The First Book of Architecture* Franklin Watts 1961 (U.S.)

Mumford, L. *From the Ground Up: Observations on Contemporary Architecture, Housing, Highway Building and Civic Design* Harcourt Brace 1965 (U.S.)

Pevsner, N. *Pioneers of Modern Design* Penguin Books 1970 (U.K. and U.S.)

Pevsner, N. *Outline of European Architecture* Penguin Books 1970 (U.K. and U.S.)

Richards, J. M. *Introduction to Modern Architecture* Penguin Books 1971 (U.K.), Barnes and Noble 1961 (U.S.)

Robertson, D. S. *Greek and Roman Architecture* Cambridge University Press 1969 (U.K. and U.S.)

Robinson, E. and P. *Houses in America* Viking 1936 (U.S.)

Rockwell, A. *Filippo's Dome* Macmillan 1968 (U.K.), Atheneum 1961 (U.S.)

Rudofsky, B. *Architecture without Architects* Doubleday 1965 (U.K. and U.S.)

Summerson, J. *Classical Language of Architecture* Methuen 1964 (U.K.), M.I.T. Press 1961 (U.S.)

Wilson, F. *What It Feels Like to be a Building* Doubleday 1969 (U.S.)

INDEX OF NAMES

designed Hagia Sophia in Constantinople for Emperor Justinian.

Apollodorus of Damascus (d. *c.* A.D. 137), Greek architect who became official architect and engineer to the Roman emperor Trajan.

Arnolfo di Cambio (*c.* 1245–1302), Florentine Gothic architect and sculptor; assistant to Nicola Pisano and master-mason of the cathedral in Florence.

Asam, Cosmas Damian (1686–1739) and Egid Quirin (1692–1750), Bavarian brothers and Baroque architects who worked together; they were disciples of Bernini north of the Alps.

Asplund, Gunnar (1885–1940), Swedish architect who integrated modern structural principles with a romantic feeling for Scandinavian national elements.

B

Barry, Sir Charles (1795–1860), British architect in the Gothic style; he collaborated with Pugin on the Houses of Parliament in London.

Behrens, Peter (1868–1940), German painter and architect who designed factory buildings and led the way to rational collaboration between architect and industry.

Benedetto da Majano (1442–97), Italian Renaissance sculptor and architect; follower of Brunelleschi; architect of the Palazzo Strozzi in Florence.

Berg, Max (1870–1947), German Expressionist architect who used reinforced concrete in undulating forms.

Berlage, Hendrikus Petrus (1856–1934), Dutch architect and town planner. Feeling his ways towards Functionalism, he still drew on historical precedents for many of his forms.

Bernard of Clairvaux, Saint (1090–1153), French ecclesiastic; persuasive advocate of simplicity in church buildings and decoration.

Bernini, Gianlorenzo (1598–1680), Italian sculptor, architect and painter; he succeeded Maderna as architect of St Peter's where he designed the colonnade; creator of the luxuriant and sensual Roman Baroque.

Bibiena, Italian family of architects, artists and stage designers in the 17th and 18th centuries; founded by Ferdinando (1657–1743).

Blondel, Jacques-François (1705–74), French; a minor architect but important theorist of neo-Classicism.

Bogardus, James (1800–74), American inventor of metal-framed buildings.

Bonaventura, Saint (1221–74), Italian scholastic philosopher who laid down rules for the building and decoration of Franciscan churches.

Bonnano de Pisa (12th cent.), Italian sculptor and architect; builder of the Leaning Tower of Pisa.

Borromini, Francesco (1599–1667), Italian architect; designer of imaginative and exuberant Baroque structures.

Boullée, Etienne-Louis (1728–99), French Romantic-Classical architect and teacher; he designed unbuildable schemes which he bequeathed to the state.

Bramante, Donato (1444–1514), Italian High Renaissance architect and painter who laid the foundations of Mannerism.

Breuer, Marcel (b. 1902), Hungarian architect and designer. A pupil of Gropius, he designed the first tubular metal furniture. Originally a Rationalist but now more arbitrary.

Brown, Lancelot "Capability" (1715–83), British architect and landscape gardener. He designed several Palladian country houses but many more parks, particularly Blenheim.

Brunel, Isambard Kingdom (1806–59), British engineer and designer of bridges, railroads, ships, etc.; he built the iron Clifton suspension bridge over the River Severn in Bristol.

Brunelleschi, Filippo (1377–1446), Italian; main architect of the transition from Gothic to the Renaissance.

Burlington, Richard Boyle, 3rd Earl of (1694–1753), British architect, arch-Palladian and generous patron of other architects.

Burnham, Daniel Hudson (1846–1912), American architect and town planner who, with Root, built the first New York skycraper, the Flatiron Building, in 1902; involved in the planning of Washington D.C. and consultant on planning for San Francisco and other American cities.

C

Callicrates (5th cent. B.C.), Greek architect who collaborated with Ictinus in designing the Parthenon; also probable builder of Temple of Athena Nike in Athens.

Callimachus (late 5th cent. B.C.), Greek sculptor; supposed inventor of the Corinthian capital.

Campbell, Colen (1676–1729), British Palladian architect, he published

Vitruvius Britannicus in 1715, reinforcing the Classical style in England.

Candela, Felix (b. 1910), Spanish engineer and architect who works in Mexico; uses reinforced concrete structures resourcefully and imaginatively.

Carloni, Italian family of artists and craftsmen working in Austria and south Germany from the 15th to the 18th centuries. Among the many members are Giambattista (d. 1657), noted for his stucco work; and Carlo Antonio (d. 1708), the most important, whose masterpiece is the Baroque Priory Church of St Florian on the Danube in Austria.

Chalgrin, Jean François Thérèse (1739–1811), French neo-Classical architect of the Arc de Triomphe in Paris which tends towards the Romantic-Classical in style; at one time a pupil of Boullée.

Churriguera, Spanish family of sculptors and architects including three brothers José Benito de (1665–1725), Joaquín (1674–1724) and Alberto (1676–1750). They gave their name to *Churriguesque*, a style overflowing with Gothic, Baroque and Moorish elements.

Chute, John (1701–76), English neo-Gothic architect who helped convert Horace Walpole's Strawberry Hill into the most influential early Gothic revival building in England.

CIAM (Congrès Internationaux d'Architecture Moderne), the focal group that sought to bring together all who worked for an architecture of the present (1928–49).

Comacini, members of the Italian Comacene guild of builders, stonemasons and sculptors which flourished from the 7th to the 14th centuries.

Cosmati, Italian guild of marble workers which flourished from the 12th to the 14th centuries particularly around Rome and in southern Italy.

Costa, Lucio (b. 1902), Brazilian architect, planner and architectural historian. He won the competition in 1957 for the design of Brasilia, the new capital of Brazil, on which he worked with Niemeyer.

Cuypers, Petrus Josephus Hubertus (1827–1921), Dutch architect who built mainly in the neo-Gothic style, with the exceptions of the Rijksmuseum and Central Station in Amsterdam which he executed in Dutch brick Renaissance.

D

Delorme, Philibert (c. 1510–70), French architect who popularized Mannerist forms without losing touch with sound medieval tradition. Author of two books which influenced French architects of his time.

Dientzenhofer, a large family of Baroque architects which worked in Germany and Bohemia, including Georg (d. 1689), who designed the Cistercian abbey church at Waldsassen; Johann (c. 1665–1726), son of Georg, architect of the Benedictine abbey church at Banz and of Schloss Weissenstein at Pommersfelden; his brother Leonhard (d. 1707), who also worked at Banz on the buildings; Kilian Ignaz (1689–1751), nephew of Johann, who settled in Prague.

Doesburg, Theo van (1883–1931), Dutch painter, sculptor and architect. With Mondrian and van Tongerloo he founded the magazine *De Stijl* in 1917 and became spokesman of the movement associated with it.

Dudok, William Marinus (b. 1884), Dutch architect and town planner; he was one of the first Rationalists.

Durand, J. N. L. (1760–1834), French architect and writer. A pupil of Boullée, his public lectures diffused advanced ideas.

E

Eames, Charles (b. 1907), American architect and designer famed for his design of mass-produced furniture and domestic objects.

Eiffel, Alexandre-Gustave (1832–1923), French engineer who built many bridges and other iron constructions but whose best-known work is the tower in Paris which he built for the Paris exhibition of 1889 and which was named after him. Made entirely of iron, for many years it was the tallest building in the world.

Elia da Cortona (c. 1171–1253), Italian architect and Vicar General of the Friars Minor, it was he who caused the Basilica of St Francis at Assisi to be built with splendour instead of in the spirit of poverty.

Elias of Dereham (d. 1245), English priest and designer of the Gothic Cathedral at Salisbury.

Endell, August (1871–1925), German architect and designer in the Art Nouveau style, who worked in Munich.

Eudes de Montreuil (1220–89), French architect; his churches and castles in the Holy Land introduced Gothic architecture there.

F

Filarete, Antonio Averlino (c. 1400–69), Italian Renaissance sculptor and architect; author of a book which included plans for a complex Utopian city, Sforzinda.

Finsterlin, Hermann (b. 1887), German painter, designer and architect who sketched unbuildable Expressionist fantasies.

Fioravanti, A. (1415–86), Italian architect; introduced Renaissance forms to Moscow.

Fischer, Johann Michael (c. 1691–1766), German Rococo architect; his decorative use of light complementing the structure of the walls, is typical of Bavarian Rococo.

Fischer von Erlach, Johann Bernhard (1656–1723), Austrian Baroque architect in the very grand manner. Court architect in Vienna, his masterpieces are the Karlskirche and the Hofbibliothek in the Hofburg there. Author of a history of architecture which included Egyptian and Chinese buildings, and had a great effect on later styles.

Fontaine, Pierre François Leonard (1762–1853), French neo-Classical architect who worked with Percier on many buildings for Napoleon.

Fontana, Domenico (1543–1607), Italian architect and engineer; chief architect to Pope Sixtus V (1585–90). He drew up ambitious proposals for the restoration of Rome.

Fourier, François Marie Charles (1772–1837), French social scientist and reformer whose ideas on Utopian communities foreshadowed Le Corbusier's *unite d'habitation*.

Freyssinet, Eugène (1879–1962), French architect and engineer, one of the first to use bearing surfaces of reinforced concrete.

Fuller, Richard Buckminster (b. 1895), American inventor of the geodesic dome, a new building form which uses tetrahedrons to make spheroid structures which combine spaciousness and economy.

G

Gabriel, Jacques-Ange (1698–1782), French architect in the Classical style, he was Premier Architect to Louis XV. He reacted to Rococo with a serene Classicism and worked principally on various royal palaces although he also designed the Place de la Concorde in Paris.

Garnier, Charles (1825–98), French 19th-century architect who employed the Baroque style for his designs for the Opéra in Paris and the Casino at Monte Carlo.

Garnier, Tony (1869–1948), French architect who produced a plan for an industrial city of 35,000 inhabitants—still considered a key work of modern town planning.

Gaudi, Antonio (1852–1926), Spanish architect who fused Art Nouveau, Gothic, Baroque, Moorish and African elements into original forms of his own.

Gerhard (13th cent.), French Gothic architect; first builder of Cologne Cathedral.

Gilly, Friedrich (1772–1800), imaginative German architect who, with his father (David Gilly, 1748–1808), upheld Classicism in Prussia.

Giulio Romano, G. Pippi (1499–1546), Italian painter and architect; pupil of Raphael and one of the most important Mannerist artists.

Gropius, Walter (1883–1969), German architect. A pupil of Behrens, he became leader of the Rationalists and founder of the Bauhaus. He sought an architecture appropriate to an industrial civilization.

Guarini, Guarino (1624–83), Italian priest, mathematician and architect. His design of the dome of the church of San Lorenzo in Turin shows his love of mathematics and a Spanish-Moorish influence. In spite of lapses, a key figure in European Baroque.

Guimard, Hector (1867–1942), French architect and sculptor in the Art Nouveau style. He designed the exterior of many Metro stations in Paris.

H

Haring, Hugo (1882–1958), German architect who adapted Expressionism to the teachings of Frank Lloyd Wright.

Harrison, Peter (1716–75), British architect who emigrated to pre-Revolutionary America where he spread Palladianism.

Haussmann, Baron Georges-Eugène (1809–91), lawyer and town planner who gave Paris its present luxurious, monumental appearance.

Herrera, Juan de (1530–97), Spanish Classicist architect; known for his work on the Escorial. Chief architect to King Philip II.

Hildebrandt, Johann Lukas von (1668–1745), Italian-born Austrian Baroque architect who became Imperial Court Engineer in Vienna; architect of the Belvedere palace and the Piaristenkirche in Vienna.

Hippodamus (5th cent. B.C.), Greek architect; originated the town plan based on right-angle axes and planned Piraeus and the city of Rhodes.

Hoffman, Josef (1870–1956), Austrian architect, pupil of Otto Wagner, he sought a romantic revival of craftsmanship.

Hood, Raymond Mathewson (1881–1934), American architect of the McGraw-Hill skyscraper in New York and the Tribune Tower in Chicago.

Horta, Baron Victor (1861–1947), Belgian Art Nouveau architect who used his highly inventive decorative style with rational building processes.

Howe, George (1886–1955), American architect, one of the most delicate architects of the 1930s; influenced by Frank Lloyd Wright.

I

Ictinus (5th cent. B.C.), Greek architect, with Callicrates designed the Parthenon. Also designed temple to Demeter and Persephone at Eleusis.

Iofan, B. M. (b. 1891), Russian architect and town planner, he built the Soviet pavilions at the World Fairs in Paris (1937) and New York (1939).

Isidore of Miletus (6th cent. A.D.), Byzantine architect who collaborated with Anthemius of Tralles in building Hagia Sophia.

J

Jacobsen, Arne (1902–71), Danish painter, architect and designer; his work was influenced by American Rationalism but modified by a crafts tradition.

Jefferson, Thomas (1743–1826), American legislator, economist, educationalist, third President of the United States, and also an architect in his own right. He established neo-Classicism as the proper architecture for the United States. He designed the Capitol building for Virginia and had a hand in planning the new federal capital in Washington from 1790 onwards.

Jenney, William Le Baron (1832–1907), American architect. By his use of iron skeleton construction, he became the "father" of modern skyscrapers. He built the first true skyscraper construction, the Home Insurance Building in Chicago, in 1883–85.

Johnson, Philip (b. 1906), American architect and town planner, a pupil of Mies van der Rohe; drastically Formalist.

Jones, Inigo (1573–1652), British architect and stage designer, he introduced Palladio to the British Isles but was far ahead of his time with his Classical buildings.

Juvarra, Filippo (1676 or 78?–1736), Italian architect and stage designer who cleverly amalgamated Baroque with Classicism. Official architect of Victor Amadeus II of Savoy, in 1735 he went to Spain where he designed the Royal Palace in Madrid, built after his death.

K

Kahn, Louis (b. 1901), American architect and town planner; brings touches from the past into his Rationalism.

Kent, William (1684–1748), British artist and architect whose elegant houses were inspired by Italy. He was an enthusiast for the natural garden.

L

Labrouste, Henri (1801–75), French architect; among the first to build in cast iron, as in the Bibliothèque Nationale in Paris.

Lanfranco, (11th–12th cent.), Italian architect; master of the Romanesque, as demonstrated by Modena Cathedral.

Latrobe, Benjamin (1764–1820), American architect whose background was European. He spread Classicism in America and worked on the Capitol in Washington. Also an engineer, he worked on river navigation and docks.

Laugier, Marc-Antoine (1713–69), French Jesuit priest and neo-Classical theorist. Advanced the idea of Functionalism; praised the "science" of Gothic while condemning its decorative features. Author of *Essai sur l'architecture* which states his Rationalist view of Classical architecture.

Laurana, Luciano (1420–79), Italian architect; disciple of Brunelleschi and Alberti; architect of the Ducal Palace at Urbino.

Le Corbusier, Charles-Edouard Jean-neret (1887–1965), Swiss architect, painter and designer, he was a decisive figure in the movement for a rational functional architecture.

Ledoux, Claude-Nicolas (1736–1806), French Romantic-Classicist architect with a social conscience, he started as a conventional architect but his designs became highly eccentric.

L'Enfant, Pierre Charles (1754–1825), French architect and planner who went to the new United States where he designed the old City Hall in New York and surveyed the site and made the plan for the new federal capital in Washington, based on Versailles.

Le Nôtre, André (1613–1700), French landscape architect and planner; also inventor of the formal "French garden", model for Europe's most famous gardens. His gardens include Versailles, Kensington Gardens, London, and the Vatican, Rome.

Leonardo da Vinci (1452–1519), Florentine painter, sculptor, engineer, scientist and architect whose brilliant studies afford glimpses of novel ideas on architecture, civil engineering and town planning.

Lescaze, William (1896–1970), Swiss Rationalist architect who worked in the United States.

Lescot, Pierre (*c.* 1510–78), French architect; considered the founder of the Classic school in France.

Lethaby, William Richard (1857–1931), British architect and writer. Joint founder of the London Central School of Arts and Crafts (1896), his writings prepared the ground for the functionalism of the 1920s.

Le Vau, Louis (1612–70), leading French Baroque architect whose main works were the château of Vaux-le-Vicomte and the remodelling of the palace of Versailles where none of his work has been left untouched.

Lissitzki, El (1890–1941), Russian painter and Constructivist architect who had links with Western Functionalists.

Lodoli, Carlo (1690–1761), Italian priest and architectural theorist whose rationalist ideas were published after his death.

Lombardo, Italian family of sculptors and architects of the 15th and 16th centuries, including Pietro (1435–1515), a pioneer of the Renaissance in Venice; his sons, Antonio (*c.* 1458–*c.* 1516) and Tullio (*c.* 1455–1532).

Loos, Adolf (1870–1933), Austrian architect and writer who reacted against Art Nouveau, proclaiming a sternly anti-ornamental doctrine.

Lutyens, Sir Edwin (1869–1944), British architect. Untouched by the Modern Movement, his best buildings in an original style triumphantly closed the phase of traditionalism in English architecture, particularly typified by the Viceroy's House at New Dehli.

M

Machuca, Pedro (d. 1550), Spanish painter, sculptor and architect who worked in Italy and then introduced Italian Renaissance forms into Spain. His masterpiece was the Palace of Charles V in the Alhambra at Granada.

Mackintosh, Charles Rennie (1868–1928), British architect, painter and designer—an isolated but influential force on European groups, he used Art Nouveau decorative features.

Maderna, Carlo (1556–1629), Italian architect; exponent of the Roman Baroque, he succeeded Fontana as architect of St Peter's, Rome.

Maillart, Robert (1872–1940), Swiss engineer; daring innovator in bridge building, he invented structural forms in reinforced concrete that were to become typical.

Malevich, Kazimir Severinovich (1878–1935), Russian painter and architect, identified with the ultramodern school.

Mansart, Jules Hardouin (1646–1708), French Baroque architect and planner, nephew and collaborator of François Mansart (1598–1666) with whom he invented the mansard roof. His main works are the Place Vendôme in Paris and his unfortunate alterations and extensions to Versailles. In his later works he veered toward Rococo.

Markelius, Sven (b. 1889), Swedish architect and town planner. City architect of Stockholm between 1944 and 1954 when he designed the plan of a new suburb, Vallingby.

MARS (Modern Architecture Research Society), group of architects who fought for Rationalism in Great Britain, extending the influence of exiles like Gropius, Mendelsohn and Breuer.

Martini, Francesco di Giorgio (1439–1501), Italian painter, sculptor and architect; Renaissance artist at Siena.

Melnikov K. S. (b. 1890) Russian architect interested in "workers' clubs"; an example of his work in the West was the Russian pavilion, Decorative Arts Exhibition, Paris 1925.

Mendelsohn, Erich (1887–1953), German Expressionist architect and writer—notably the Einstein Tower at Potsdam.

Meyer, Adolf (1881–1929), German architect who collaborated with Gropius.

Michelangelo Buonarroti (1475–1564), Italian genius of the High Renaissance, who built as sublimely as he worked as poet, painter and sculptor.

Michelozzo di Bartolomeo (1396–1472), Florentine sculptor and architect; one of the principal architects of the early Renaissance.

Mies van der Rohe, Ludwig (1886–1969), German architect whose "stripped-down" aesthetic is expressive in its generous use of space and sumptuous use of material and has innumerable imitators.

Milizia, F. (1725–98), Italian writer whose critical writings, especially his rejection of Michelangelo and Borromini, stirred up controversy throughout Europe.

Morris, William (1834–96), British designer and writer who influenced architects. He affirmed the unity of all art forms and the architect's social responsibility; founder of the Arts and Crafts movement.

Muthesius, H. (1861–1927), German atchitect and writer. Active in the German Werkbund, he worked for an interrelationship of industry and art, through which the architect would foster prosperity and peace.

N

Nash, John (1752–1835), British architect who was also an inspired town planner—Regent's Park and Regent Street (latter destroyed). He designed Buckingham Palace but was dismissed from the work on the death of George IV.

Nervi, Pier Luigi (b. 1891), Italian engineer whose superb structures, based on his own hypotheses checked in practice, constitute an architecture that is the product of computation.

Neumann, Johann Balthasar (1687–1753), German Rococo architect; imaginative and theatrical Baroque designer of the pilgrimage church of Vierzehnheiligen.

Neutra, Ricard (1892–1970), Austrian architect and writer who settled in the United States where he worked mainly on private housing, in an "organic Rationalism".

Niemeyer, Oscar (b. 1907), Brazilian architect and town planner; adapts Le Corbusier's "module" to the tropical landscape; inclines towards Expressionist forms; worked with Costa on the Brasilia scheme.

O

Olbrich, Joseph Maria (1867–1908), Austrian architect, pupil of Otto Wagner and one of the founders of the Secession movement in Vienna—a group sympathetic to modernist tendencies in the applied arts.

Oud, Jacobus Johannes Pieter (1890–1963), Dutch modernist architect, a leader of the *de Stijl* group. City architect of Rotterdam where he specialized in workers' housing schemes.

Owen Robert (1771–1959), British social reformer, planner and pioneer who devoted his wealth and energies to the creation of conditions that would harmonize industry with a decent life.

P

Pagano, G. (1896–1945), Italian architect and crusader of Rationalism in Italy.

Palladio, Andrea (1508–80), Italian architect; creator of a style based on a personal interpretation of Roman buildings. Through his writings he had a great influence on English architecture of the 18th century.

Paxton, Sir Joseph (1801–65), British self-taught architect and horticulturist, he provided the design in cast iron and glass for the Great Exhibition of 1851, the Crystal Palace.

Percier, Charles (1764–1838), French Classical architect who collaborated with Fontaine on buildings for Napoleon; a designer in the Empire style—Arc de Triomphe du Carrousel, Paris.

Perrault, Claude (1613–88), French doctor and amateur architect; influential at the court of Louis XIV. He prevailed in his arguments in favour of giving the eastern façade of the Louvre the colonnade on which Le Vau and the painter Lebrun collaborated. In 1673 he brought out an edition of Vitruvius which influenced greatly the neo-Classical revival.

Perret, August (1874–1954), French architect, engineer and town planner who used reinforced concrete.

Phidias (5th cent. B.C.), Greek sculptor; directed the rebuilding of the Acropolis.

Piermarini, Giuseppe (1734–1808), Italian neo-classical architect and planner. He worked mainly in Milan and was the architect of Teatro della Scala (the opera house).

Pierre de Montreuil (or Montereau, c. 1200–67), French master-mason of Notre Dame; also designed the High Gothic transept and nave of St Denis, Paris.

Piranesi, Giambattista (1720–78), Italian painter, engraver and architectural theorist. In his immensely popular etchings he interpreted Roman remains in a spirit of moody romanticism and had a strong influence on the development of neo-Classicism and Romanticism.

Pisano, Italian family of architects and sculptors which flourished from the 13th to 14th centuries. Nicola (d. 1280), introduced Gothic forms into central Italy; Giovanni (c. 1250–c. 1314) was master-mason of the cathedrals at Siena and Pisa.

Poelzig, Hans, (1869–1936), German Expressionist architect of the Grosses Schauspielhaus in Berlin.

Ponce de Milgueil (11th cent.), French Romanesque architect who designed the third abbey of Cluny, the greatest church of the Middle Ages.

Ponti, Gio (b. 1891), Italian architect and designer, originally influenced by the Secession but latterly an International Modernist. His finest building is the Pirelli skyscraper in Milan.

Pöppelmann, Mathaeus Daniel (1662–1736), German Baroque architect. His Zwinger palace at Dresden is a Rococo masterpiece.

Pozzo, Andrea dal (1642–1709), Italian Jesuit priest, architect and painter working in Rome and Vienna; his ceiling paintings were illusionist and influenced European architecture.

Pugin, Augustus Welby Northmore (1812–52), English architect and propagandist of the Gothic revival, demonstrated by his Gothic details in the façades and interior fittings of the Houses of Parliament on which

he collaborated with Sir Charles Barry.

Q

Quadrio, G. B. (d. c. 1590), Italian Renaissance architect who worked in Poland.

Quarenghi, Giacomo (1744–1817), Italian neo-Classical architect who worked in Russia in a pure Classical style at St Petersburg.

R

Raphael Sanzio, (1483–1520), Italian painter and architect; key artist of the High Renaissance.

Rastrelli, Bartolommeo Francesco (1700–71), Italian Rococo architect who worked in Russia where he counts as the founder of Baroque. His best known works are the Winter Palace and the Great Palace (Tsarskoe Selo), now the Pushkino, in St Petersburg.

Richardson, Henry Hobson (1838–86), American architect who rejected current revivals in the United States and whose use of simple forms points towards Rationalism and the development of an independent American style.

Rietveld, Gerrit Thomas (1888–1964), Dutch architect of the *De Stijl* school. His most famous building is the Schroeder House in Utrecht.

Rinaldi, Antonio (c. 1709–90), Italian Late Rococo architect who worked in Russia where he introduced the use of marble facing.

Roebling, John Augustus (1806–69), American engineer; brilliant constructor of suspension bridges built with continuous elastic steel wire ropes.

Rondelet, J.–B. (1743–1829), French architect and writer; disciple of the neo-Classicists Lodoli and Laugier's teaching.

Root, John Wellborn (1850–91), American architect who worked with Burnham.

Rossellino, Bernardo (1409–64), Italian sculptor and architect whose main works were the palace and cathedral at Pienza.

Rudolph, Paul (b. 1918), one of the most advanced American architects, he was a pupil of Gropius.

Ruskin, John (1819–1900), British art critic and sociological writer; the strongest literary influence on attitudes to architecture in his time. He promoted the revival of medieval styles for modern purposes.

S

Saarinen, Eero (1910–61), Finnish architect who worked mainly in the United States in the International style, approaching Expressionism—an example is the TWA terminal at Kennedy Airport, New York.

Salvi, Niccolo or Nicola (1697–1751), Italian Late Baroque architect and designer of extravagant decorations for festivities, particularly the Trevi Fountain in Rome.

Sangallo, Italian family of architects and sculptors of the 15th and 16th centuries; including Giuliano da (1445–1516), architect, sculptor and military engineer who assisted Raphael on designs for St Peter's; Antonio the Elder (c. 1455–1534), brother of Giuliano, also an architect and military engineer; and Antonio the Younger (1483–1546), his son, also an architect and military engineer and who also worked with Raphael.

Sanmicheli, Michele (1484–1559), Italian architect and military engineer; a leading Mannerist architect in Venice.

Sansovino, Jacopo (1486–1570), Italian architect and sculptor; an outstanding figure in Venetian Renaissance architecture.

Sant'Elia, Antonio (1888–1916), Italian architect influenced by the Secession but basically a Futurist.

Scharoun, Hans (b. 1893), German Expressionist architect of the Philharmonic Concert Hall, Berlin.

Schinkel, Karl Friedrich (1781–1841), German painter, neo-Classical architect and planner; a pupil of Gilly, he was the Romantic interpreter of the theories of Ledoux and a forerunner of the Modern movement.

Scott, Sir George Gilbert (1811–78), British architect who supported and was a chief exponent of the Gothic revival, using it for churches, stations and, in particular, the Albert Memorial in London.

Semper, Gottfried (1803–79), German architect and writer. In spite of his preference for historical styles, his architecture was based on functional ideas, as in the Burgtheater in Vienna.

Serlio, Sebastiano (1475–1554), Italian architect and writer on art; helped to spread Mannerism in France.

Sert, José Luis (b. 1902), Spanish

architect, town planner and writer; a pupil of Le Corbusier and now working in the United States.

Shaw, Richard Norman (1831–1912), British architect identified with the "Queen Anne revival" in England.

Sher Shar Sur (16th cent.), Indian architect and town planner.

Shreve, R. H. (1877–1946), American architect who worked on the Empire State Building in New York.

Siloe, Diego de (c. 1495–1563), Spanish architect and sculptor; leading representative of Italian High Renaissance and decorative art, the Plateresque.

Sinan, Mi'mar (1489–1578/88), Turkish architect who considered his best work to be the Selimiye mosque at Edirne (Adrianople). Also famed as a mathematician.

Soane, Sir John (1753–1837), British neo-Classical architect with a taste for the Middle Ages. His London house, containing his collections, was left to the nation and is now a museum. He designed the Chelsea Hospital.

Soufflot, Jacques Germain (1713–80), French neo-classical architect, designer of the Panthéon, Paris.

Starov, Ivan Yegorovich (1743–1808), the first Russian-born neo-classical architect, his masterpiece is the Tauride Palace in St Petersburg.

Stone, E. D. (b. 1902), American architect of the Museum of Modern Art in New York.

Suger (1081–1151), French; abbot of St Denis, adviser to the king of France, promoter of crusades and the man behind the politico-religious programme that launched Gothic art and architecture.

Sullivan, Louis Henry (1856–1924), American architect who became the leader of the Chicago School.

T

Tange, Kenzo (b. 1913), Japan's greatest living architect, his early work, like that of many others, was influenced by Le Corbusier.

Tatlin, Vladimir E. (1885–1953), Russian architect of the Constructivist movement.

Taut, Bruno (1880–1938), German Expressionist architect. Pioneer of the use of glass, he worked in Russia, Japan and Turkey.

Telford, Thomas (1757–1834), British engineer and bridge builder who worked in a variety of materials; his main work was the Menai suspension bridge, built of iron.

Thornton, William (1759–1828), American architect and designer; for a time the supervisor of construction of the Capitol in Washington, he also designed a number of private houses there.

Toledo, Juan Bautista de (d. 1567), Spanish Classical architect, philosopher and mathematician who worked on the Escorial.

U

Utzon, Jorn (b. 1918), Danish Expressionist architect of Sydney Opera House.

V

Valadier, Giuseppe (1762–1839), Italian archaeologist, town planner and architect; a Romantic interpreter of neo-Classicism, his main work was the Piazza del Popolo in Rome.

Vanvitelli, Luigi (1700–73), Italian painter and architect whose design for the palace at Caserta was the last great Italian Baroque building. He marked the transition from the Baroque to neo-Classical.

Vasari, Giorgio (1511–74), Italian Mannerist architect; designer of the Uffizi; founder of modern art history and criticism.

Velde, Henri van de (1863–1957), Belgian architect prominent as an Art Nouveau designer in the German Werkbund.

Vesnin, Russian brothers; Leonid (1880–1933), architect and town planner; Viktor (1882–1950) architect; Aleksandr (1883–1950) architect and stage designer.

Vicat, L.-J. (1786–1861), French engineer who studied hydraulic lime, the basis of modern concrete.

Vignola, Giacomo da (1507–73), Italian Mannerist architect and architectural theorist; succeeded Michelangelo as chief architect of St Peter's; designer of the church of the Gèsu in Rome which had great influence.

Villard de Honnecourt (13th cent.), French architect whose *Notebook* illustrates aspects of cultural life in the Gothic period.

Viollet-le-Duc, Eugène-Emanuel (1814–79), French architect and authority on Gothic art. Controversial restorer of notable Romanesque and Gothic buildings in France.

Vitruvius Pollio, Marcus (1st cent. B.C.), Roman architect and engineer; author of a treatise, *De Architectura,* which decisively influenced the Classical revivals of the Renaissance and later.

Voysey, Charles F. Annesley (1857–1941), British architect and designer of unassuming rural houses, the white surfaces and apparent simplicity of which persuaded Muthesius and many continental architects that he was a Rationalist at heart—which Voysey denied.

W

Wagner, Otto (1841–1918), Austrian architect who progressed from Baroque forms through Art Nouveau to Functionalism.

Wilkins, William (1778–1830), British architect of the Greek revival, as exemplified by the National Gallery in London.

William de Ramsey (d. 1349), English architect; master-mason of St Paul's and Lichfield Cathedrals.

William of Sens (d. c. 1180), French designer and master-mason who worked on Canterbury Cathedral.

Winckelmann, Johann Joachim (1717–68), German archaeologist and art critic; the principal theorist of neo-Classicism he was inspired by an ideal of Greek beauty.

Wood, John, the elder (1704–54), British architect and town planner; disciple of Palladianism. He planned the town of Bath but his scheme was only partly executed. His work was continued by his son John Wood the younger (1728–81),

Wren, Sir Christopher (1632–1723), British architect and planner. His rational and far-seeing plan for rebuilding London after the great fire of 1666 was not adopted, but he took part in the reconstruction, building or repairing of many churches. His masterpiece was the rebuilding of St Paul's Cathedral—Classical in style but with Baroque influences in the detail.

Wright, Frank Lloyd (1869–1959), American architect and writer. The greatest exponent of "organic" architecture, the stylistic incoherence of his enormous output has given him no followers.

Z

Zevi, Bruno (b. 1918), Italian architect and town planner; author of *History of Modern Architecture.*